M000203053

ASTON MARTIN
DB4, DB5 & DB6

Other titles in the Crowood AutoClassics Series

AC Cobra	Brian Laban
Alfa Romeo: Spider, Alfasud & Alfetta GT	David Styles
BMW M-Series	Alan Henry
Ferrari Dino	Anthony Curtis
Jaguar E-type	Jonathan Wood
Jaguar XJ Series	Graham Robson
Jensen Interceptor	John Tipler
Lamborghini Countach	Peter Dron
Lotus Elan	Mike Taylor
Lotus Esprit	Jeremy Walton
Mercedes SL Series	Brian Laban
MGB	Brian Laban
Porsche 911	David Vivian
Sporting Fords: Cortina to Cosworth	Mike Taylor
Sprites and Midgets	Anders Ditlev Clausager
Triumph TRs	Graham Robson

ASTON MARTIN DB4, DB5 & DB6

The Complete Story

Jonathan Wood

First published in 1992 by
The Crowood Press Ltd
Ramsbury, Marlborough
Wiltshire SN8 2HR

© The Crowood Press Ltd 1992

All rights reserved. No part of this publication may be reproduced or transmitted in any form or by any means, electronic or mechanical, including photocopy, recording, or any information storage and retrieval system, without permission in writing from the publishers.

British Library Cataloguing in Publication Data

A catalogue record for this book is available from the British Library.

ISBN   1 85223 447 4

Picture Credits

The photographs in this book were kindly supplied by the National Motor Museum's Motoring Picture Library, Beaulieu.

Typeset by Chippendale Type Ltd, Otley, West Yorkshire.
Printed and bound in Great Britain by BPCC Hazells Ltd.
Member of BPCC Ltd.

Contents

The Aston Martin DB4, DB5 and DB6 in Context

Pre-production

1955   July: John Wyer appointed Aston Martin's technical director.
        August: Tadek Marek begins design of DB4 engine, DP 186.
1956   Spring: Harold Beach starts work on DP 184, the definitive DB4.
        July: John Wyer appointed Aston Martin's general manager.
        November: DB4 engine runs for first time.
1957   July: First DB4 prototype, DP 184/1, completed.
        August–September: John Wyer takes prototype on Continental tour.

Production Cars

1958   October: DB4 launched at the Paris and London Motor Shows.
1959   October: DB4 GT announced.
1960   October: DB4 GT Zagato introduced at London Motor Show.
1961   October: DB4 convertible announced; Lagonda Rapide saloon launched at
        London Motor Show.
1963   July: DB5 production starts.
        September: John Wyer leaves to join Ford.
1965   October: DB5 convertible becomes Volante; DB6 introduced.
1966   October: DB6 Volante announced; DBS two-seater displayed at Paris and London
        Motor Shows.
1967   October: Towns-styled six-cylinder DBS announced.
1969   July: DB6 Mark II announced.
        October: V8-engined DBS announced.
1970   November: DB6 Mark II ceases production.
1972   February: Sir David Brown sells Aston Martin to Company Developments.
        May: six-cylinder AM Vantage introduced.
1973   July: AM Vantage ceases production.

Acknowledgements

Over the years I have much enjoyed talking to individuals associated with the Aston Martin and Lagonda concerns, but I should like to single out two in particular who, in their respective spheres, were responsible for greatly increasing my knowledge of the company and its cars. Aston Martin's chief engineer Harold Beach provided me with a fascinating insight into the evolution of the DB4 and its successors, while specialist Richard Williams contributed much helpful information relating to the purchase of a DB4, 5 or 6. However, I am alone responsible for any conclusions reached in this book.

Particular thanks are also due to the Aston Martin Owners' Club and its secretary Jim Whyman. Not only was a copy of that mine of information, the Club's *Register*, made available to me, but I also owe a great debt of gratitude to Brian Joscelyne, editor of the Club's excellent *AM Magazine*, for his permission to quote extracts from that publication.

I would like to record my appreciation to Shaun Campbell, editor of *Autocar & Motor*, for his permission to reproduce road test reports of Aston Martins of the 1958 to 1970 era.

Jonathan Wood

1 Birth of a Thoroughbred

'One of the greatest of all sports cars, the Aston Martin was
scarcely ever made in any other form.'
William Boddy, *The Sports Car Pocketbook* (Batsford, 1961).

The Aston Martin DB4 which appeared in 1958 was rightly hailed as the finest British Grand Tourer of its day and would, over the next seven years, pave the way for its DB5 and DB6 successors. But above all, it represented the ultimate expression of a sports car line that had begun forty-five years previously.

To discover the origins of one of Britain's most famous sporting marques, we must return to 1914. It was on 9 May of that year that Lionel Martin, a wealthy Old Etonian whose family had made its money through Lincolnshire granite quarries, completed a successful ascent of the half-mile Aston Martin hill climb, located in the Chiltern Hills of Buckinghamshire. Driving a specially tuned Singer Ten on handicap, he achieved a victorious run. At this time he was planning to produce his own car – is it too fanciful to suppose that it was after this victory that he decided to call his car an Aston Martin, so uniting his own name with the location of his latest triumph?

Lionel Martin was a partner in the firm of Bamford and Martin, a London garage which he had established with his friend Robert Bamford in 1913. Soon to be housed at Henniker Place, South Kensington, London, the firm held a sub-agency for the popular Singer car and Martin's competitive activities had begun after he had bought one of the firm's best-selling 10hp cars at the 1912 Motor Show. His mechanic, Jack Addis, was able to tune it so that it would be capable of 70mph (113kph) rather than its more staid 40mph (64kph). The little car, with its sporty external exhaust pipe, was to prove its worth in rallies and hill climbs and, before long, Lionel Martin received requests for replicas.

Rather than market a Singer-based car, however, Martin opted for one of his own design. This was to be powered by a proprietary 1,400cc side valve Coventry Simplex engine though the chassis would be purpose built. Impatient to try his new creation, and still awaiting delivery of a new chassis, he installed the engine in a frame from a small Isotta Fraschini of the type that had competed in the voiturette race at Dieppe in 1908. It was completed in time for Martin to compete in the Brighton Speed Trials which took place a few weeks before the outbreak of the First World War. The onset of hostilities temporarily put a stop to the project, although the prototype, curiously known as the 'Coal Scuttle', was on the road in March 1915 and by June 1919 had covered around 15,000 miles (24,139km).

PRODUCTION BEGINS

With the coming of peace, Lionel Martin decided to press ahead with his car project. A second prototype was built in 1920 though later, in 1921, Robert Bamford decided to withdraw from the firm. His place as director was taken by Martin's wife, Katherine.

Lionel Walker Birch Martin (1878–1945)

Lionel Martin, who gave his name to the marque, was born into what his biographer A.B. Demaus, *Lionel Martin, A Biography* (Transport Bookman 1980) describes as 'comfortable circumstances', thanks to the family mining and quarrying business of Singleton Birch Ltd. The Aston Martin was created for rich young men like himself, who were more interested in a car's performance than its cost. During his school-days at Eton between 1891 and 1896 he became a keen cycling enthusiast and pursued this when he went up to Oxford, continuing to race two- and three-wheelers until 1912. He seems to have first become involved with the motor car from late 1903 when he joined forces with a cycling friend to sell De Dion Bouton and Napier cars, and spent some years demonstrating them throughout the United Kingdom.

In January 1913 Martin began selling Calthorpe, G.W.K. and Singer cars with his friend Robert Bamford from premises in Callow Street, Fulham Road and this led to the Aston Martin car which absorbed much of his fortune. The firm went into a receivership on 11 November 1925 but two days later, on 13 November, the receiver Arthur Whale dispensed with Lionel Martin's services. At around this time, the Hon. John Benson, a fellow director, was heard to make some critical remarks about Martin and the latter sued him on seven counts of slander. The case was heard in October 1926 and although Martin won, he was awarded a derisory ¼d damages on each count which amounted to 1¾d in all.

From thereon, Martin retired from active competition although in 1928 he was elected a member of the British Racing Drivers' Club. He drove a Humber Snipe in the 1933 Monte Carlo Rally, and he and his wife participated in that year's Alpine Trial. Martin continued to enjoy his motoring, owning Rileys, two 18/80 MGs, no less than eight Wolseley Hornets, a Railton and a 328 BMW, but no Aston Martins. During the Second World War he once again reverted to pedal power and enjoyed riding a tricycle. On 14 October 1945 he was on his trike when he was knocked down by a car near his Kingston-on-Thames home. He died a week later, on 21 October, at the age of sixty-seven.

By this time the firm had moved to 53 Abingdon Road, Kensington, London, and Martin had the assistance of Jack Addis and S. Robb, a draughtsman who had been involved with the design of the Coventry Simplex engine that had powered the first car.

The Aston-Martin car (the name was hyphenated on and off until the David Brown take-over of 1947) entered production in 1,487cc form in 1923 and was to remain virtually unchanged until 1925, by which time about fifty-three examples had been built. In its standard form, the Robb-designed four developed a modest 38bhp, although it was available in two chassis lengths and the shorter sports version had a 45hp engine.

In addition to the mainstream Aston Martin, some special competition cars were taking shape behind the scenes. Addis had built a short chassis one called 'Bunny' in 1921, in fact the third and final prototype, and, in the following year, it broke the test hill record at Brooklands. A single overhead camshaft car did not come up to expectations, but, at around this time the Polish Count Zborowski, creator of the legendary aero-engined 'Chitty Chitty Bang Bang', asked Martin to build a special twin overhead camshaft engined racing car which he could run in the 1922 French Grand Prix to be held near Strasbourg. He supplied the firm with £10,000 to undertake this work and two cars were built though neither did well and retired early on.

By 1924 Aston Martin had consumed approximately £100,000 in developing new cars – a not inconsiderable sum and a small fortune by the standards of the day. Inevitably

The date is 24 May 1922 and the location Brooklands track. Sammy Davis is at the wheel of 'Bunny', the special Aston Martin which that day collected a batch of world records. It was also driven by Bertie Kensington Moir, (left) and Clive Gallop, who is in front of the car. Lionel Martin is standing with his back to the camera.

The first Aston Martins were produced by Lionel Martin between 1921 and 1925. This long-wheelbase example, registered XT 1979, was delivered to its first owner, the Revd Capt. Ward, as a four-seater tourer in 1924. It was then rebodied as this open two-seater by Jarvis of Wimbledon.

this financial drain was beginning to strain even Martin's well-lined pocket. He had managed to interest Lady Charnwood in the firm as her son, the Hon. John Benson, had joined Martin and his wife on the board of directors. Benson had read engineering at Oxford and was anxious to try his hand at car design – the outcome was another costly twin overhead camshaft engine which was exhibited at the 1925 Motor Show, staged at Olympia. Aston Martin was displaying its products there for the first time and it looked like being the last because on 11 November, within a few weeks of the event closing, Bamford and Martin was in receivership. Lionel Martin severed his connections with the car that bore his name and thereafter he concentrated his activities on the family granite business.

UP FOR SALE

Benson's father, Lord Charnwood, bought the assets of Bamford and Martin but was uncertain how next to proceed. The receiver decided to put Aston Martin up for sale and he was no doubt surprised at the amount of response it generated – not only did Vauxhall and the Bristol Aeroplane Company show interest, but so did the French Donnet et Zedel company. However, it was not a car manufacturer but a private individual who effectively put money into Aston Martin. His name was William Sommerville Renwick and his firm of Renwick and Bertelli was, with Charnwood, to own equal parts of a new company named Aston Martin Motors. Renwick had inherited a family fortune and at the time was working for Armstrong Siddeley at Coventry. He had met Augustus Cesare 'Bert' Bertelli there, who was to be responsible for the design of every production Aston Martin built between 1926 and the outbreak of the Second World War. Bertelli had enjoyed a variety of jobs prior to meeting up with Bill Renwick in Coventry –

during the First World War he had worked for Graham White Aviation at Hendon, although after hostilities he moved to Birmingham to work for the Enfield Allday company. This firm was committed to producing a curious rear-engined car and, although Bertelli wasted little time in pointing out the errors of their ways and designed a more orthodox 10hp car, it came too late. The firm went broke and he found himself out of a job. There then followed a spell when he worked as a freelance designer in and around the car companies of Birmingham and Coventry. He did this until he had the good fortune to be taken up by millionaire Woolf Barnato, who commissioned a purpose-built car from him – three Bertellis were constructed although they ran without success in the 1923 200 Miles Race at Brooklands. This proved a short-lived venture and, during a visit to Armstrong Siddeley, Bertelli met Renwick and the latter proposed that he and Bert build their own car. Despite Renwick's fortune, Bertelli considered that they did not possess sufficient funds to become full-scale car producers, but wisely suggested that the two make their own proprietary engine which could then be sold to the motor industry.

They accordingly set up the firm of Renwick and Bertelli with a factory in the Tyseley district of Birmingham, and the duo designed a four-cylinder 1½-litre single overhead camshaft engine. This was a sensible decision because most proprietary engines of the day were low-powered, side valve units. To evaluate their new creation they produced a single car which was nicknamed the '*Buzz Box*'.

NEW OWNERS

Renwick and Bertelli then received an approach from the Hon. John Benson of Aston Martin, and they travelled south to London and viewed the Kensington garage

Aston Martins of the Bertelli era pictured at the Light Car Club's Relay race at Brooklands in 1936. Left to right: D. Campbell's car and 'Mort' Morris-Goodall and C.M. Anthony, who won at 87.91mph (141.47kph).

where the cars had been built. They decided to go ahead and invest in the firm, Renwick putting up the money which, in truth, only represented the Aston Martin name. Most importantly though, the business was moved from the capital to the Middlesex suburb of Feltham. There, at Victoria Road, Aston Martin was established in part of a works that had previously been used for the manufacture of Whitehead aircraft – it was destined to remain Aston Martin's home for the next twenty-one years. In addition, Bert's brother Enrico (who was known as Harry) established an adjacent coach-building facility, although from 1929 E. Bertelli Ltd. became separately owned and would not only body many Aston Martins but also provide coachwork for other makes of car.

The first of a new generation of Aston Martins made its début at the 1927 Motor Show. Low, purposeful and fast, it was built around the 1½-litre four-cylinder overhead camshaft engine, and perpetuated the concept of an expensive, low production sports car which had been established by Lionel Martin.

But there were more corporate upheavals in the offing. Benson and Lord Charnwood departed, and in 1928 the firm was reconstructed as Aston Martin Ltd. S.C. Whitehead came in as chairman and Renwick left in 1931 to go off to America. The firm's position at this time was extremely vulnerable, a state of affairs that had been exacerbated by the 1929 Wall Street Crash. Support came and went, and Aston Martin was not placed on a sound footing until 1932. In that year it was bought by the Newcastle shipping magnate, Sir Arthur Munro Sutherland Bt., for his son, Robert Gordon Sutherland, to manage. The latter was only in his twenty-fourth year at the time and he was to share the joint managing directorship of the company with Bert Bertelli.

Despite these uncertainties Bertelli revived the practice of entering works cars in important races from 1928. Not only did such events provide excellent publicity but any shortcomings that exposed themselves could be rectified on the production cars. Two Aston Martins ran at Le Mans in 1928 and, apart from 1929, 1930 and 1934, the marque appeared in the 24-hour classic event for every year until 1964, which was an unparalleled record for a British manufacturer. In 1931 the make was placed fifth and it succeeded in attaining similar positions in 1932 and 1933. Even greater success came in 1935 when an Aston Martin achieved a third place at Le Mans, a considerable achievement for the product of a relatively small car company and the best it would attain in the inter-war years. Nearer home, Aston Martin achieved a class victory in the 1931 Tourist Trophy race. In 1934 the firm won the team award, a success which paved the way for the legendary short chassis, tuned Ulster, which was one of the truly great British sports cars of the pre-Second World War era.

BERTELLI DEPARTS

The cars had evolved in Mark II form for 1935 but, despite the fact that they sold better than any previous model, Sutherland was anxious to broaden the appeal of the company's products. With the arrival of the 15/98 in 1936, not only was the four's capacity increased to 2 litres, but the emphasis was switched to touring cars and saloons (although some open two-seaters were built). However, there were problems when the larger capacity engine proved to be a rougher runner than its predecessor, ironically a shortcoming which was more apparent by the use of closed coachwork. Bertelli and Sutherland clashed over what Bert believed was a dilution of the company's sporting pedigree and he left Feltham early in 1937. He thereafter devoted himself to farming and became a successful pig breeder.

With Bertelli's departure, his assistant Claude Hill, who had also worked for Renwick and Bertelli, took over design responsibility and he was soon at work on what would eventually form the basis of the next generation of Aston Martins. In 1938 came a curious looking saloon, nicknamed 'Donald Duck' with a box section chassis, and next during the same year the C-type, distinguished by a cowled radiator and modern bodywork, its chassis being equally advanced and made of square section tubing. These exercises paved the way to Hill's experimental car, which was called the 'Atom' because it was said to have 'lots of power in a small package'. It was a much more sophisticated design than Bertelli's earlier Aston Martins for, unlike these cart-sprung predecessors, it was fitted with coil-sprung trailing link independent front suspension which required as rigid a chassis as possible. Hill therefore opted for a robust frame made of square and rectangular tubing. The four-cylinder theme of the earlier cars was perpetuated, initially with a 2-litre 15/98 engine, although this was later replaced by Hill's new unit, also a four but with pushrods taking the place of the costly single overhead camshaft. A Cotal electric gearbox, a fashionable feature for the day, was also fitted. The concept of the closed body was perpetuated, and this also had the virtue of being more aerodynamically efficient than its open-top counterpart. Completed in mid-1940, both Hill and Sutherland put in around 100,000 miles (160,093km) in the 'Atom' both during and shortly after the War. During the conflict,

Aston Martin produced aircraft parts and, with the coming of peace, it emerged in good financial shape.

ENTER DAVID BROWN

What happened next is best told in Sutherland's own words (as recounted in 'My Sixty Years of Motoring', *AM Magazine*, Spring, 1985):

By 1947, therefore, we were ready technically to produce a completely new Aston. Also, after continuous war work, our financial position for the first time since 1934 was sound, and we had a better machine shop and equipment than ever before. The Company was now totally mine, all the share capital having been sold to me by my father at a nominal figure. I still hold the receipt dated 23 October 1944 for £5! To launch into production was, however, going to need much more money than I personally could risk, and I could hardly approach my father again after his generosity.

Sutherland therefore took the rather unusual, though as it transpired, very prudent step of placing an advertisement declaring his intention, in the personal column of *The Times* under a box number. His idea was to see if he could find a 'suitable' person to take the company over:

Of the several replies I received, that of David Brown really interested me, as here was someone with the engineering connections as well as capital. I therefore approached him and showed him all our new designs, as well as letting him try the 'Atom'.

Sir David Brown (born 1904)

Although David Brown was forty-three when he bought Aston Martin and Lagonda in 1947, his Yorkshire-based gear manufacturing business had been involved in motor car manufacture from before the First World War. In 1908 David Brown Ltd of Huddersfield began manufacturing the appropriately named two-stroke Valveless car and, from 1910, it also built a Renault look-alike named the Dodson. In the same year it obtained the British concession from the Belgian S.A.V.A., which was noteworthy because it was the firm's first involvement with a sporting marque.

All these activities ceased with the outbreak of hostilities in 1914. After the war the firm continued its association with the industry and, as a component supplier, it specialized in manufacturing worm drive gearing for rear axles. There was a further involvement in competition when, in the late 1920s, the firm made the supercharger gearing for Raymond Mays's Vauxhall Villiers hill climb car, and was also responsible for the manufacture of the Roots supercharger for the rare and delectable Squire sports car of the 1934 to 1936 era.

David Brown's grandfather (also David) had founded the firm in 1860, and the young David Brown joined as an apprentice in 1921. His father, Frank Brown, became ill in 1928 and when his uncle Percy died in 1931, David Brown was appointed joint managing director with former works manager W.S. Roe. Unfortunately within six weeks of the appointment Roe became ill and died in August 1932, leaving David to take over the running of the company at the tender age of 28. The decade was to be difficult for the firm, but it was also to be one of expansion. David Brown Foundries was established in 1935 and David Brown Tractors in 1939, and all the businesses were brought under the umbrella of the David Brown Organization in 1951.

Brown was knighted for services for export in 1968. But by the late 1960s his business was beginning to experience liquidity problems which culminated in Sir David selling Aston Martin to Company Developments in 1972. The still sprightly Sir David lives in retirement today in Monte Carlo.

David Brown bought Aston Martin in 1947 and owned it until 1972. This portrait appeared in the David Brown Corporation's official history, published in 1960.

The millionaire industrialist gave the car a demanding road test in the Pennines and has since said that while he thought its road-holding was excellent, he considered it underpowered and thought the closed body rather ugly. Sutherland continued:

It was apparent straight away that he was extremely interested, but in true Yorkshire fashion he negotiated cautiously. Our actual assets, machine tools etc., at a write down value were worth £21,000, quite apart from any goodwill or the new designs. His meagre offer of £14,000 horrified me; but he did seem the ideal person to take over the company and develop it into something worthwhile.

Several weeks of haggling followed but as Sutherland recalled:

Bearing in mind the future of the enthusiastic employees . . . I decided I must seize this chance which seemed to offer such great possibilities. Actually we finally settled at a figure of £20,500, with an agreement that Claude Hill and I stay on as technical directors.

The purchase was made by David Brown personally, and not his company, in February 1947 and, while Hill did remain at Feltham for a time, Sutherland was to leave. As it happened, he had purchased Friary Motors of Old Windsor with the intention of developing it into Aston Martin's service and experimental department. It was agreed that he retain this, and he also took over the pre-war Aston Martin spares and drawings as well as the 'Atom' saloon which by then had outlived its usefulness. Later, in 1950, Sutherland purchased the E.D. Abbott coach-building concern of Farnham, Surrey which had also produced some Aston Martin bodies before the war.

AND THEN LAGONDA

David Brown's ownership of Aston Martin was followed later in the year by his purchase of the Lagonda company. Built at nearby Staines, cars of that name had been produced from 1906 and, in 1935, the bankrupted firm had been purchased by a consortium headed by the London solicitor, Alan Good. A new generation of models had been produced, namely the celebrated V12 which appeared in 1937 and its LG6 associate. Despite these new cars Good, like Sutherland, had recognized the changing circumstances of the post-war world. Lagonda had therefore developed a new design during the war which was the work of no less a personage than W.O. Bentley, whom Alan Good had brought to

Lagonda as its technical director when he took control of the firm. W.O., with the assistance of William Watson and Donald Bastow, had produced an advanced car with a cruciform chassis, all independent suspension and significantly powered by a purpose-designed 2.6-litre six-cylinder twin overhead camshaft engine. Although five prototypes had been built, the all-new Lagonda did not enter production. Announced in September 1945, it was planned to begin manufacture in 1946. The engine, it should be noted, was designated the LB6 (for Lagonda Bentley).

However, when the car was advertised as the 2½-litre Lagonda-Bentley, Rolls-Royce (which owned the Bentley name) not surprisingly took exception. A court case which was held in December 1946 decided in Rolls-Royce's favour, and the episode is said to have cost Alan Good about £10,000. There were further problems: a shortage of steel and the fact the Briggs Motor Bodies, which had quoted to produce the bodywork, was unable to undertake the work because of other commitments. Good therefore decided to devote his energies to promoting a consortium devoted to the manufacture of diesel engines, and needed to sell the Lagonda car but not the Staines factory where it had been manufactured.

Soon after he had bought Aston Martin, David Brown was approached by Tony Scatchard, who managed the Lagonda distributor in Bradford. He brought news that at a meeting he had attended of the firm's distributors it was revealed the company was in financial difficulties. He pleaded with Brown to buy the business, but the industrialist was reluctant because he knew it would stretch his personal resources – he had, it will be recalled, purchased Aston Martin with his own money. By this time Lagonda had a new chairman in the shape of J.R. Greenwood, who had taken over from Alan Good in March 1947. By chance, Brown already knew Greenwood from when he had been running the Craven Machine Tool Company. Out of little

more than curiosity, David Brown approached him and then visited Staines. Arriving by aircraft, he was met at London Airport by W.O. Bentley in one of the Lagonda prototypes. However, he soon learnt that offers in the region of £250,000 were necessary to secure Lagonda, and the company had already received three (from Armstrong Siddeley, Jaguar and Rootes), and the price was far beyond anything that he could contemplate. Nevertheless, he drove one of the prototypes and was immediately attracted to the potential of its engine which he thought would make an ideal new Aston Martin unit. Claude Hill was anxious to develop a six-cylinder version of his 2-litre pushrod four, but Brown had vetoed the idea and told him that he could not afford to put it into production.

A BARGAIN BUY

David Brown informed Greenwood that in view of the asking price he could not consider buying Lagonda, though he did leave a bid of £50,000 before his departure. Soon afterwards, however, the Chancellor of the Exchequer, Sir Stafford Cripps, made one of his gloomy financial prognostications and, in consequence, the three offers for Lagonda were withdrawn. Greenwood therefore approached David Brown and told him that he had received two revised bids though they were substantially less than the original ones. Brown once again returned to the Staines factory and to Greenwood's office. The Lagonda chairman then tactfully left the room, having deposited the documents relating to the two offers he had received open on his desk. Brown needed little prompting to notice that the higher of the two offers was £50,000, and he immediately put in a bid of £52,000 – Lagonda was his. As the news was announced in September 1947, it was within the space of only eight months that David Brown had bought two of Britain's most famous makes for a total of £72,500.

One of the conditions of the agreement was that all the Lagonda plant had to be removed from the Staines factory within six weeks, because it had been sold to Good and his associates to manufacture Petter diesel engines. Brown was due to leave the country on the following day, so he telephoned James Whitehead (his manager at Aston Martin), told him what he had done and asked him to find premises which were near enough to Staines to keep the Lagonda workforce intact. Whitehead was able to find some hangars at the Hanworth Air Park, only half a mile from Aston Martin's Victoria Road factory. Fortunately many key personnel from the Staines company were to join Aston Martin. Most significant was the firm's talented stylist, Frank Feeley, who had the superlative coachwork of the pre-war V12 Lagonda to his credit. His colleague, Frank Ayto, who had also worked on that illustrious model, went to Feltham as chief draughtsman.

In buying Lagonda, David Brown was able to implement a three-fold objective. Not only did he want Bentley's engine for the Aston Martin, but he was also intent on putting the Lagonda car into production – initially it was produced in small numbers until 1957. Brown was determined now to pursue an active competition programme and also he recognized that although the new engine would be ideal for a road car, it could also form the basis of a racing unit.

DEVELOPMENT OF THE 'ATOM'

In the meantime at Feltham, Claude Hill

The Belgian 24-hour race, held at Spa in July 1948, was the first event of this duration to be won outright by Aston Martin. The DB1 was driven by St John Horsfall and Leslie Johnson, seen here at the wheel. Their winning speed was 71.84mph (115.61kph).

had been developing the concept of the 'Atom'. The wheelbase was extended to 9ft (2,743mm) though the tubular frame was retained. The front suspension evolved and was a coil spring and trailing arm unit, coils also being used on the live rear axle. The Cotal gearbox was replaced by a four-speed unit built by David Brown. Road evaluation was undertaken by the seasoned Aston Martin racing driver, St John 'Jock' Horsfall, who joined the firm as tester. In May 1948, the car was driven by Joseph Lowry, technical editor of *The Motor*, who reported that:

There are few cars in which I like to drive quickly until I have settled down after a substantial mileage – but on this occasion I almost immediately found myself storming considerable corners at speeds in the seventies or above.

While this car was evolving, work was also underway on a lightened, racing version which was entered for the 24-hour race at Spa, to be held in July 1948. The idea had been Horsfall's and the entire car was built in a mere nine weeks and completed just in time to compete in the final practice session. Driven by Horsfall himself and Leslie Johnson, the car won an event in which only twenty-three of the forty entries were still running. After many years of competing at Le Mans, it was the first occasion that an Aston Martin had won a 24-hour race outright. Needless to say Claude Hill, who witnessed the victory, was delighted at the endorsement of his engine and chassis.

THE DB1 ARRIVES

Three months later, the road version of the car was displayed at the 1948 Motor Show. Titled the 2-litre 'For the Sportsman', it was

The first Aston Martin of the David Brown era, the 2-litre Sports, retrospectively titled the DB1. Announced at the 1948 London Motor Show, it was powered by a four-cylinder pushrod engine and only fourteen examples were built between then and 1950.

The shape of things to come. One of three DB2s which ran at Le Mans in 1949, driven by T.A.S.O. Mathieson and Pierre Marechal

fitted with an open two-door, three-seater body. Styled by Frank Feeley, he had originally conceived the lines for the V12 Lagonda but the concept had been vetoed by W.O. Bentley. David Brown had decided against the closed bodywork of the 'Atom' and wanted to revert to an open one to perpetuate the spirit of the pre-war cars. However, the car was expensive at £2,331 and a mere fifteen examples had been built by the time that production ceased in May 1950. This model has been retrospectively named the DB1 (for David Brown) but, by this time, it had been replaced by the DB2, the first of a Grand Touring line and a concept which would be perpetuated in the DB4 of 1958.

2 A Grand Tourer in the Making

'My first assignment after my appointment as Technical Director in July 1955 was for a car, or a range of cars, to replace the existing Aston Martin and Lagonda.
John Wyer 'The Development of the DB4', AM Magazine, Spring, 1990.

When the DB2 was announced in the spring of 1950, it represented not only a new type of Aston Martin, but the firm was one of a few British car makers to take up the *Gran Turismo* concept which had been gaining ground in post-war Italy. This was at a time when most British sports cars were invariably open two-seaters in the manner of their predecessors, while a GT meant a closed, high-performance car as this type of bodywork was more aerodynamically efficient than an open one with less wind resistance and, consequently, greater speed. Aston Martin thereafter became firmly wedded to the Grand Touring theme and remains so to this day.

In the years between 1923 and 1939, the firm had built around 700 cars which reflected its relatively small-scale operation. With the resources of David Brown and Sons behind it, Brown was not only able to increase production carefully, he was also able to build up the racing programme with the twin-fold objective of winning the Mille Miglia and the Le Mans 24-hour race. He was to achieve the latter ambition, though the former eluded him.

Inevitably, Brown's purchase of Lagonda caused problems at Feltham. Claude Hill continued work on the six-cylinder version of his sturdy pushrod four but this was a paper project. By contrast, the Lagonda engine already existed, had been tested, was running and was the reason for Brown buying the firm. Hill was understandably disappointed that his six was to be sidelined and he left Feltham in April 1947 after a furious row with David Brown. Hill later became chief engineer of Harry Ferguson Research which was engaged in pioneering four-wheel drive work. St John Horsfall had departed at the end of 1948 and was tragically killed in August of the following year when his ERA crashed at the British Racing Drivers' Club Silverstone meeting.

A RACING START

What was effectively the prototype DB2 made its début at the 1949 Le Mans 24-hour race – the first to be held after the War. John Eason-Gibson was appointed team manager and three cars were prepared which were based on what had been the concept of the 'Atom' chassis fitted with a completely new and stylish two-door coupé body designed by Frank Feeley. Two cars were powered by Hill's pushrod four, although under the bonnet of one was the Lagonda 2.6-litre six. None of this trio did particularly well at the Sarthe circuit. One of the Hill-engined cars, driven by Arthur Jones and Nick Haines, came in seventh while the other crashed and its driver, Pierre Marechal, was badly injured and died the following day. He was

The DB2, as it originally appeared in 1950, powered by the 2.6-litre twin overhead camshaft six-cylinder Lagonda engine and with the fine lines of its Frank Feeley styled body readily apparent.

to be the only fatality Aston Martin was to experience in fifteen years of racing. The Lagonda-engined car, in which Leslie Johnson and Charles Brackenbury were to share the driving, dropped out after six laps with water pump trouble. Later at the Spa 24-hour race, it proved its worth and was third with the same drivers, and the other pushrod-engined car came in fifth.

BRITAIN'S GRAND TOURER

The DB2 proper made its début in April 1950. Unquestionably its most impressive feature was its bodywork which closely resembled that of the Le Mans-prepared cars of the previous year, although the production version was slightly wider and with increased head room. A distinctive feature was the bonnet and front wings which was a single unit hinged at the front. Opening it would not only reveal the engine but also the front suspension. Such was the competence of Feeley's work that many believed that the car had been styled in Italy. Made of aluminium on a steel frame, these bodies were built at Feltham. There was also a more traditional drophead coupé which, in this initial stage of DB2 production, would account for about a third of output.

With the DB2, the concept of the 'Atom' chassis was perpetuated, but the wheelbase, at 8ft 3in (2,446mm), was 9in (23cm), shorter than that of the DB1, although in other respects it resembled it. In place of Hill's four was the Lagonda engine, a 78 × 90mm unit of 2,580cc which developed 100bhp at 5,000rpm with a modest 6.5:1 compression ratio. It had a cast-iron block/crankcase and head while the crankshaft ran in four main bearings. These were contained in split annular aluminium housings or 'cheeses' which were located by hollow dowels in the crankcase and held firm by expansion. W.O. Bentley had, incidentally, first noticed the feature in the French Chapuis-Dornier car of pre-First World War days. The twin overhead camshafts were chain driven while the valves operated at an included angle of 62 degrees. The small 10mm sparking plugs were an unusual feature and had been adopted so as not to unduly restrict water passages in the head. Drive was taken to the rear axle via a gearbox built by David Brown which had synchromesh on second,

third and top gears. The coil-sprung axle was secured by trailing radius arms with a Panhard rod to check lateral movement. Brakes were all-round Girling hydraulics.

On announcement the DB2 was marketed for £2,331. By its nature it was an expensive car and, to give this price some perspective, it could easily have bought two examples of Jaguar's new XK 120 sports car, which at the time, interestingly, was also powered by a new twin overhead camshaft six-cylinder engine. Production got under way and was essentially an assembly operation. The engine, gearbox and chassis came from factories within the David Brown group and they were united with the Feltham-built coachwork in a single large hangar in the Hanworth Air Park. Finished cars were eventually being built at the rate of about one a week.

A 1953 DB2, pictured at the by then derelict Brooklands track. It remained available in this form until the spring of that year.

An Aston Martin in its element, a DB2–4 drophead coupé for 1954, photographed outside the Hotel Carlton at Cannes. This is in fact the right-hand drive works demonstrator LML 588.

THE VANTAGE OPTION

When *The Autocar* came to road test an early DB2 later in 1950, it achieved a top speed of 110mph (177kph). Its driver found the close ratio third gear to be remarkably effective and the DB2 attained a speed of 96mph (154kph) before he had to change into top. The model's handling came in for fulsome praise, and the only jarring note was represented by the brakes which tended to suffer from 'pedal judder and some front end vibration when full braking was laid on at high speed'. Towards the end of 1950 came a more powerful version of the twin cam six in the shape of the Vantage engine with an 8.2:1 compression ratio, instead of the customary 6.3:1. This was to be a feature of Aston Martin models from then on.

In the same year in which the DB2 appeared, Aston Martin had a new racing manager in the shape of John Wyer. Already a dedicated motor racing enthusiast, he had joined the Monaco Motor and Engineering Company of Watford, Hertfordshire in 1947 as managing director. Established before the War by Peter Monkhouse and Ian Connell, Monaco specialized in the preparation of racing cars, and later, in 1948, Connell's place was taken by Dudley Folland.

John Leonard Wyer (1909–1989)

If any one person can have been responsible for bringing the DB4 to fruition, it was Aston Martin's general manager, John Wyer, who had joined the firm in 1950 as competitions manager.

A life-long motor racing enthusiast, his father was the Sunbeam distributor in Kidderminster, and it was while young John was at his prep school that he picked up a copy of *The Autocar* and saw a photograph of Kenelm Lee Guiness driving a 350bhp Sunbeam in a race against Count Zborowski. From thereafter his passion for trains was relegated to second place by his fascination for motor sport. In February 1927 he therefore joined Sunbeam at nearby Wolverhampton as a premium apprentice because it was the only British company to be involved in motor racing – even though it had withdrawn from competition at the end of the previous year. Wyer completed his apprenticeship in 1932 and became a design draughtsman with the firm. However, Sunbeam was clearly in deep financial trouble by then, so he left and obtained a job with the London-based Solex Ltd in its technical sales and service department. Soon afterwards he was sent by the carburettor company to India, returning in about 1937. During the Second World War Wyer was in charge of production and material control. It was from there that, in 1947, he went to Monaco Engineering which led him to join Aston Martin.

After thirteen years with the company he left in 1963 and became managing director of Ford Advanced Vehicles and, as such, played a key role in the GT 40 programme whose aim was to win the Le Mans 24-Hour Race. Later he and John Willment formed J.W. Automotive Engineering and its Gulf racing GT40s won Le Mans in 1968 and 1969. This was to lead to a two-year contract with Porsche to run the new 917 sports racers, the cars winning eleven out of seventeen races, although tantalizingly not Le Mans. Wyer's company won Le Mans again, however, for the fourth and final time with a Gulf Mirage in 1975.

Wyer and his family retired to the south of France but later moved to America. He died at his home in Scottsdale, Arizona aged seventy-nine.

At this time Folland was running a pre-war 2-litre Aston Martin which Monaco prepared for the 24-hour race at Spa, the same event, it will be recalled, that Aston Martin successfully fielded its lone DB1. It was also the first occasion that John Wyer had been involved in entering and supervising the running of a car in an international competition. The old Aston Martin initially ran splendidly until Connell, who was co-driver, spun off the road after over twelve hours of running. Then, in 1949, John Wyer received an approach from W.F. Spurling of the London-based Spurling Motor Bodies who wanted to buy Monaco and make it part of an expanding Vauxhall dealership. Wyer first turned the offer down, although he recognized that the days of a business such as Monaco must be numbered. He named a substantially higher figure to which Spurling later agreed and Wyer thereupon informed Monkhouse and Folland that he had sold the company!

WYER AT FELTHAM

It was then that John Wyer heard from Laurence Pomeroy, the respected technical editor of *The Motor* and confidant of David Brown, that Aston Martin was looking for a new racing manager. By all accounts there had been an uneasy relationship between Brown and John Eason-Gibson and, unbeknown to Wyer, Brown had been impressed with how he had run Folland's pit at Spa. There followed an interview and the Aston Martin chairman informed him that he would be only required for a single season. Wyer was, however, to remain with the firm for the next thirteen years, first as racing manager, then technical director and finally as general manager.

Meanwhile, the Aston Martin road car line was continuing to evolve. By April 1953 a total of 309 examples of the original DB2 had been built and there were a further 100 or so drophead coupés. There then followed a six-month hiatus before the DB2–4 replacement appeared at the 1953 Motor Show, because of changes in the cars' manufacturing procedure. Aston Martin had had its fair share of labour problems at Feltham and in-house bodywork was becoming increasingly expensive to produce. The outcome was that David Brown decided to stop producing coachwork for road cars though racing bodies continued to be constructed on the premises. The contract for the new DB2–4 body was therefore awarded to a specialist body builder, in this instance, Mulliners of Birmingham, which was the largest of Britain's smaller body-makers and which already undertook work for Standard Triumph, Daimler, Rootes and Alvis. The coupés were manufactured at its Bordesley Green works and then transported to Feltham for final assembly.

MORE ROOM

The Aston Martin DB2–4 generally followed the lines that Frank Feeley had established with the DB2, and was so called to reflect the fact that four passengers could now be carried. In truth, this really meant two adults and two children and was created in response to requests from owners with growing families who wanted to continue Aston Martin motoring. All the firm's subsequent Grand Tourers would be equipped in this way. The car's wheelbase remained the same though the pedals, steering wheel and front seats were modified to permit the introduction of new, small rear seats.

Luggage carrying capacity was also improved by removing the cross-bracing above the rear axle so that the petrol tank could be relocated between the side members, although this did mean reducing the tank's capacity from 19 to 17 gallons (86 to 77 litres). The car's tail was accordingly extended by about 6in (152mm) and there was a useful rear opening door to load the luggage. When the rear seats were not occupied, the back also folded down to form an enlarged platform. It was probably the first time that a production high-performance car had been so equipped and has since been widely copied, most noticeably in Britain by Jaguar for its E-type coupé of 1961 and the MGB GT three years later.

Mechanically the car closely resembled that of its DB2 predecessor although that model's Vantage engine was standardized in view of its greater weight. The DB2–4's top speed of 110mph (177kph) was about the same but its acceleration was inferior to that of the DB2. This shortcoming was remedied in April 1954 when the 2–4 was fitted with an enlarged, 3-litre version of the twin cam six which had first appeared in a Feltham-built road car under the bonnet of the exclusive Lagonda saloon the previous year.

A RACING COMMITMENT

To trace the origins of the 3-litre unit, we must briefly retrace our steps to chart the progress of the firm's racing programme. It was to provide Aston Martin with invaluable publicity and culminated in the firm winning the prestigious World Sports Car Championship in 1959, making it the only British manufacturer to have done so. During the decade, Aston Martin and the Coventry-based Jaguar Cars were the country's principal exponents of sports car racing, though their respective approaches to competition could not have been more divergent. While David Brown was a motor racing enthusiast through and through, and campaigned his cars for the sheer fun of it, spending approximately £2 million in the process, Jaguar's William Lyons pursued racing for the hard-headed, single-minded objective of winning the famous Le Mans race to provide a formidable spur to sales of his profit-making and mainstream saloon car range.

Also, in John Wyer David Brown had chosen an outstanding team manager, and, in 1960, the Aston Martin chairman paid this tribute to him:

I have now been to hundreds of motor races with John Wyer and we have spent the long hours together at Le Mans. I have seen him in the early hours of the morning when vitality is at its lowest and bad temper at its highest; he is always calm and clear in his decisions.

Wyer was not the only new recruit to arrive at Feltham in 1950. Towards the end of the year, Robert Eberan von Eberhorst joined the company as chief engineer. Once again it had been Laurence Pomeroy who had effected the introduction. However, in retrospect, David Brown looked upon the appointment as a mistake and, as he told Chris Nixon in *Racing with the David Brown Aston Martins* (Transport Bookman, 1980), 'he pushed von Eberhorst down my throat, telling me how wonderful were his designs for Porsche and Auto Union'. But Brown found that he was 'living in the past . . . he was too cautious.'

There was little doubt that the Austrian engineer had impeccable technical credentials for the appointment. A racing enthusiast from his youth, he had studied in Vienna until 1927, and then had moved to Germany and been assistant at the Technical Institute in Dresden. In 1933 he was asked by Ferdinand Porsche, who was in the process of designing the revolutionary mid-engined P-Wagen for Auto Union, to join the firm to undertake testing and vehicle development. This he did

under the direction of Auto Union's Dr Werner, and in Porsche's absence in 1938 and 1939, he was responsible for the P-Wagen's more successful D-type derivative. In 1940 von Eberhorst returned to Dresden and, at the end of the War in 1945, he escaped from the Russians and went to Italy to become involved with Ferry Porsche's Cisitalia four-wheel-drive Grand Prix car.

A SPORTS RACING CERTAINTY?

Through the good offices of Pomeroy, von Eberhorst had come to Britain and ERA at Dunstable, where he designed the Jowett Jupiter's distinctive tubular chassis. He was unhappy there, and when Pomeroy told David Brown of the Austrian's predicament, Aston Martin took over the remainder of his contract, and in November 1950 von Eberhorst arrived at Feltham. Although his first assignment was to update the Lagonda saloon, his appointment reflected the fact that, if Aston Martin was to remain competitive in international competition, a new purpose-designed sports racing car would have to be created, which would utilize the 2.6-litre Lagonda engine, heavy as it was. It was intended to have what was designated the DB3, ready for the 1951 season although the first example was not completed until the latter part of that year.

In 1950 John Wyer had run a trio of more or less standard DB2s at Le Mans and they had come in a very creditable fifth and seventh, and first and second in the three-litre class. The model did even better at Le Mans in the following year. Despite the fact that the DB3 had been conceived for the 1951 racing season, work was progressing too slowly for Wyer's liking, so he initiated the construction of two lightweight DB2s as it was hoped that the team would be completed by a single DB3. Both chassis were extensively drilled, the interior trim was

dispensed with, plexiglass was used for the side windows and the bodies were built of 16 rather than 18 gauge aluminium. All these modifications saved a precious 450lb (204kg), and the Weber carburettored engine developed 138bhp rather than the 124bhp of the Vantage unit. When it transpired that the eagerly awaited new sports racer would not be ready, the team was completed by a partially lightened DB2 which had run in the previous year's race.

The event proved particularly satisfactory for Aston Martin, with Lance Macklin and Eric Thompson coming in third, ironically in the 1950 car, and the lightweights fifth and seventh; the DB2s were once more first and second in the 3-litre class. Two privately entered Feltham cars finished tenth and thirteenth. This meant that five Aston Martins had started and all had finished, an achievement which did wonders for sales and the marque's growing international reputation.

THE DB3 AT LAST

The long awaited DB3 made its competition début at the Tourist Trophy race at Dundrod in September 1951. Its twin tubular chassis and trailing link independent front suspension bore a striking resemblance to von Eberhorst's pre-war D-type Auto Union, though there was never any question of the DB3 being mid-engined. There was a de Dion rear axle with inboard disc brakes, and transverse torsion bars, so beloved of Dr Porsche, were employed front and rear as the suspension medium. The engine was the 2.6-litre Lagonda unit, although the output was essentially the same as that employed in the lightened DB2s and accordingly

A DB Mark III distinguished by its revised radiator grille, echoing that of the sports racing DB3S. This and engine revisions helped it to sell 551 examples.

developed 138bhp. The open two-seater, with bodywork styled by Frank Feeley was simple and stylish. Lance Macklin drove the car in the TT, but it dropped out on the twenty-seventh lap, having run a bearing after the engine developed an oil leak.

The DB3 was to do better when a team of four cars appeared for the first time in the Silverstone race meeting of May 1952 and they took second, third and fourth places, and were first and second in the 3-litre class. The cars were running in 2.6-litre form but, at the Monaco Grand Prix of the following month, they were powered by an enlarged 3-litre engine which would eventually find its way under the bonnet of the DB2–4 road car in 1954.

It should be recalled that Jaguar was running in 3.4-litre form at this time so there was a great incentive for Aston Martin to increase the capacity of the Lagonda unit. However, this proved to be a far from straightforward operation. One of the difficulties was that the position of the main bearings meant that the cylinders were siamesed in three batches of two and the walls were not thick enough to cope with the requisite 5mm increase in bore size. This was subsequently accomplished by offsetting the liners and doing the same to the little ends of the connecting rods, however, this exerted undue bending loads on the gudgeon pins. Three of the four DB3s at Monaco – the Grand Prix was that year dedicated to sports cars – suffered connecting rod breakages, although one car continued running and finished seventh.

DISAPPOINTMENT AT LE MANS

Le Mans, held only two weeks after Monaco, was a disaster. Because of the débâcle in the south, all three cars were running in 2.6-litre form and all these dropped out, two with drive failure through faulty hypoid

gears in the rear axle and the third with water pump trouble. Fortunately the gear difficulties proved to be a one-off problem.

The unreliability of the 3-litre engine was soon resolved. Eberan von Eberhorst discovered that the answer was to offset the connecting rods at the bearing end, and all enlarged engines were thereafter so equipped. Three DB3s, powered by the revised twin cam six, ran in the Nine-Hour Race at Goodwood in August and although one retired, the other, driven by Peter Collins and Pat Griffith, won the race. The third DB3 unfortunately caught fire in the pits, an accident that put John Wyer in hospital for six weeks.

At the end of a rather disappointing year, Aston Martin was contemplating another season with the DB3. However, during the winter of 1952/53 senior design engineer, William Watson, came up with the concept of the DB3S. He had originally been involved with the design of the LB6 engine during his days at Lagonda, had gone on to create the unorthodox Invicta Black Prince, a twin overhead camshaft six-cylinder Meadows engine coupled with a Brockhouse torque converter, and had joined Aston Martin in 1952. He came up with the idea of lightening the DB3 by cranking the sides of the chassis tubes to reduce the car's height and then substituting its 16 and 14 gauge tubing with 14 and 12 gauge stock. Von Eberhorst reluctantly agreed to this proposal and the prototype DB3S was running by May 1953. The resulting car was 167lb (75kg) lighter and was both shorter and narrower than the DB3. Frank Feeley came up with a new, curvaceous body with distinctive cutaway front wings to permit hot air to escape from the engine compartment, a shortcoming that had manifested itself on the DB3.

ILL-FATED V12

However, Willie Watson had less luck with

his other assignment and that was for a new V12 Lagonda. This had been conceived by David Brown as a Ferrari beater, and the V12-engined Modena cars were running in 4½- and 4.9-litre forms at this time. Its greater capacity would also give Aston Martin the edge on the Jaguar opposition and Watson, under the overall supervision of Eberhorst, had responsibility for the concept. It was envisaged that, like the Italian cars, the V12 would be produced in road and sports racing form though, for reasons that will soon become apparent, it was only built in the latter form which was allotted the designation of DP (for Design Project) 116. Its chassis was similar to that of his DB3S but the wheelbase was increased to 8ft 4in (2,540mm). For the engine, Watson closely followed the concept of the original LB6 Lagonda unit. This meant retaining the

'cheeses' to contain the main bearings and there were seven of these rather than the four of the production six. But in the interests of weight saving, he replaced the cast-iron crankcase with an aluminium one which represented the project's undoing. On the DB2 engine, the system worked well enough because the aluminium and iron had differing coefficients of expansion and, once hot, the entire unit tightened up. But when the same principal was employed with an aluminium crankcase, which shared the same differential as the 'cheeses', it put an undue and ultimately unacceptable strain on the main bearings.

The remainder of the wet liner engine closely followed that of the existing Lagonda unit, each bank of six cylinders being fitted with alloy twin overhead camshafts heads and two plugs per cylinder in the manner of

The first purpose-designed sports racer of the David Brown era was the DB3 of 1951. Peter Collins is seen here in a sports car race at Silverstone in 1953 when the Aston Martins trounced the C-type Jaguars. He was placed second in class and fourth overall.

In 1953 the DB3 concept was lightened and modified and the resulting DB3S proved more successful than its predecessor. This example, finished in the Aston Martin team's almond green livery, is pictured at the firm's stand at the 1953 London Motor Show.

the DB3S of 1954. Watson took the opportunity of designing a more modern, short stroke, oversquare engine and the V12, in its basic 4,486cc form, had a 82 × 69mm bore and stroke. This briefly gave 312bhp rather than the anticipated 350 to 375bhp. A 4,983cc version, with 87mm liners, was also contemplated but never developed.

PRESTIGE RESTORED

While work on the V12 Lagonda was under way, the DB3S was proving its worth. DB3Ss were run for the first five months of 1953, and an example finished second in Aston Martin's Sebring race and another achieved a third place at Silverstone in May. The cars made their début at Le Mans, but

the race proved to be a disappointment because one DB3S crashed, another retired with clutch trouble and the third suffered valve problems. From then on, however, the new cars never lost a race in 1953. They won the Empire Trophy Race at Silverstone in July where the Jaguars were decisively trounced for the first time, at Charterhall, in the Goodwood Nine-Hour Race and the Tourist Trophy where a DB3S also came in second.

After such an encouraging start, the following year of 1954 was, by contrast, a disaster. The DB3Ss managed a third at Sebring and the cars took the first three places in the July Silverstone meeting, but otherwise the cars either suffered mechanical failure or crashed. The latter fate befell two specially prepared DB3S coupés and a Lagonda at Le Mans with the other two DB3Ss dropping out with mechanical trouble.

The V12 had made its début at the Silverstone meeting in May 1954 and, although it began to lose oil pressure as soon as it got hot, Reg Parnell managed to coax it into fifth place, which was the best performance by a Feltham car that day. Parnell also achieved a fourth position in the Lagonda at the same circuit in July. The following year, in an attempt to lighten the car, its DB3S-based chassis was dispensed with and replaced with Feltham's first spaceframe. Designated DP 166, the V12 ran at Le Mans in 1955, although it retired in what was its last appearance on the race-track after ninety-three laps.

LAGONDA DÉBÂCLE

Alas, the engine would never be reliable as it was designed and, whenever the alloy twelve was stripped down after a race, it was found that its Glacier bearings were in a distressed state. In 1955 the Lagonda drawings were sent to the Shoreham-based consulting engineers, Ricardo and Company which was prepared to redesign the crankcase, but it would have cost £150,000 to have got two modified engines running and, wisely, the V12 was quietly put to sleep.

The calamitous performance of the Lagonda on the race-track also scuppered any thoughts of using the engine in a road car, even though an experimental Lagonda

Had this 4.5-litre Lagonda been successful, the next generation of Aston Martin road cars might have been V12 powered. Reg Parnell pictured at the Daily Express *race at Silverstone in May 1954 when he managed a fifth placing.*

saloon had been built and was run by David Brown for some time. This was Design Project 117 and was initially the work of Eberan von Eberhorst. It had a tubular chassis with the rear suspension modified to his principles. It was dual rated and could be adjusted to varying road conditions by the employment of a hydraulic ram half-way down the torsion bar, and wishbone and coil springs were used at the front. Frank Feeley created the body which, unusually, had curved window glasses. Inevitably, a V12 Lagonda engine was never fitted and the car was powered by the current 3-litre twin cam six.

On the race-track, 1955 proved to be a better year for the DB3S. These were now developing 225bhp with their twin-plug alloy cylinder heads. Front disc brakes had arrived in 1954 and, in 1955, they were fitted all round. The cars came in first and second at Silverstone in May, and an example also came second at Le Mans behind the winning D-type Jaguar. This was the first occasion that an Aston Martin had finished the race since 1952, but it was also the year of the terrible crash which resulted in the withdrawal of the entire Mercedes-Benz team. There followed wins at Aintree, where DB3Ss took the first four places, and at Crystal Palace, in the Goodwood Nine-Hour race and at the Tourist Trophy where a car came in fourth.

WYER PROMOTED

The year of 1955 was an all-important one in Aston Martin's affairs on the corporate front, and particularly so in the light of the development of the DB2–4's successor which would finally emerge as the DB4 in 1958. In addition to the position of team manager, John Wyer was promoted in July to the newly created post of technical director with a seat on the Aston Martin Lagonda board. His first action was to separate the design of the racing and road cars; hitherto they had been produced by

the same drawing office. The Racing Design Office was to be solely responsible for the creation and development of competition cars. Eberan von Eberhorst had left Feltham at the end of 1953 and returned to Germany and the transplanted Auto Union company at Dusseldorf, where he developed the firm's range of two-stroke cars – a greater contrast to his work at Feltham is difficult to imagine! Ted Cutting, who had joined Aston Martin in 1949 and who was a member of the racing design team, was appointed to the post of chief racing designer. The creation of Aston Martin's all-new sports racer, the DBR1, was placed in his capable hands.

The Production Design Office was to be exclusively concerned with the next generation of Aston Martin road cars. At its head was Harold Beach and, in retrospect, he considers Wyer's promotion as 'the most significant in the Aston Martin story, for a true sense of direction and purpose descended on Feltham'. Beach would be responsible for engineering the DB4, 5 and 6, along with its V8 successor, and would remain with the firm, latterly in the post of technical director, until his retirement in 1978.

A NEW RECRUIT

Beach had joined Aston Martin as a design draughtsman in 1950. He had originally seen the job advertised in the *Daily Telegraph*, and was interviewed at Feltham by chief draughtsman, Frank Ayto. Yet trouble loomed when he raised the all-important matter of salary. Harold asked for £11 a week and Ayto told him that he could not possibly sanction that and Beach would have to see manager James Stirling. An interview followed which convinced Harold Beach that he would not get the job. 'They're obviously looking for a genius' he told his wife. But a few days later the firm contacted him and wanted to know when he could start . . . He recalls,

Harold Beach (born 1913)

Beach became Aston Martin's chief engineer in 1956, and had wanted to be a draughtsman since his school-days. In 1928 he began work with the respected Barker coach-building company at its North Kensington premises. After spending some time in the machine shop he finally achieved his ambition and entered the drawing office. This brought him into contact with many fine motor cars and he still recalls seeing an Aston Martin on his way to work. 'I remember thinking I'd like to own one. Of course, it was completely out of my reach, a new one would have cost about £600. Little did I realize how closely I would be associated with that famous name.'

It did not take Harold long to realize that despite its prestige, Barker was not moving with the times, so he left and joined the commercial vehicle manufacturer William Beardmore at Clapham as a draughtsman. However, he was anxious once again to become involved with cars and James Ridlington, who had run the Barker machine shop, asked Harold to join him in his own business which he called J.R. Engineering. He had bought Barker's tools, and one of Ridlington's more noteworthy assignments was to modify the 3½-litre Bentley which Eddie Hall ran in the 1934 and 1936 Tourist Trophy races. Harold was responsible for styling the car's bodywork.

With the threat of war, Beach began to look elsewhere and got a job as a designer draughtsman with another commercial vehicle manufacturer, Garner Straussler Mechanisation, in Park Royal. He remained there throughout the war and, in the late 1940s, the firm diversified into tractor production. Harold was still bent on a motor car involvement, however, and he joined Aston Martin in 1950. There his sense of purpose and quiet efficiency was soon recognized by David Brown who later said of Beach: 'I have a very high regard for him'. He was responsible for the chassis of the DB4, DB5 and DB6 and, with some regrets because it was not new, the V8's. His last assignment was engineering the Volante version which appeared in 1978, the year he retired, after twenty-eight years with the firm.

Those days at Feltham were tremendous. The standard of work in the drawing office was extremely high and there were plenty of draughtsmen, like Frank Ayto, who'd come from Lagonda and, prior to that, Bentley. They'd already produced the DB2 that really had a fantastic reputation, I think everyone else was reluctant to consider any other design.

Harold Beach's arrival brought him into close contact with chief engineer, Robert Eberan von Eberhorst: 'It was something of a young designer's dream to work with someone like that'. The first thing he did was to buy a 20in slide rule because von Eberhorst always worked to three or four decimal places!

Beach had already begun work on the DB2–4's successor in 1954 – what the new car's chassis drawings referred to as the DB4. This was titled, in corporate terms, Design Project 114/2. DP 114/1, by contrast, was probably never completed. The Claude Hill tubular chassis was dispensed with and Beach opted instead for a perimeter frame. He also did not perpetuate the trailing arm independent front suspension which had been such a distinctive feature on the Aston Martin road and competition cars. He points out that:

Although trailing arms keep the wheels vertical, there are plenty of serious disadvantages. The roll centre is at ground level and the position of the steering rack is predetermined by trailing links. But when Robert [von Eberhorst] arrived, almost the first thing he said to me was 'I see you have the only type of suspension I could contemplate'.

FIRST THOUGHTS

For his part, Beach preferred a wishbone and coil-spring layout and Project 114/2 was so equipped. At the rear, von Eberhorst's influence was more apparent because Beach echoed the Aston Martin sports racing line and adventurously chose a de Dion layout with parallel trailing links, the lower ones being connected to laminated torsion bars. The engine was the 3-litre BDA unit and the running chassis was completed early in 1956. It was fitted with a basic and very un-Aston-Martin-like angular test body, and Harold Beach covered many thousands of miles evaluating the chassis and suspension. Then came a proper four-seater coupé body and, because it was finished in white with a blue top, it was always known at Feltham as the 'Wall's ice cream van'. Registered for the road as 4 MMC in August 1957, it was thereafter used by David Brown's wife.

By this time it had been decided that Project 114 would not be the definitive DB4, part of the trouble lying in its bodywork. Whereas the car's chassis was appropriately progressive, the same could not, alas, be said

The Mark III's coachwork was by Tickford. David Brown having bought the firm in 1954.

The W.O. Bentley designed Lagonda six-cylinder twin overhead camshaft engine which had been enlarged from 2.6 to 3 litres in 1954 and revised by Tadek Marek for the Mark III.

Driving compartment of the DB Mark III. The Grand Touring theme would be perpetuated on the DB4.

The Mark III's new instrument panel, the layout of which was carried over for the DB4 and through to the DB6.

for its appearance. Frank Feeley had come up with a characteristically competent design though it lacked the flair that he had expended on the DB2, and drew on previous inspirations that accordingly took little account of contemporary design trends.

In 1956 there came yet another change in the firm's corporate hierarchy with John Wyer's appointment as general manager. He immediately strengthened Harold Beach's hand by appointing him chief engineer. Clearly Wyer could not also continue with the job of racing manager and his place was taken by former Aston Martin racing driver Reg Parnell, the two working well together in an atmosphere rooted in mutual respect.

By this time a Mark II version of the DB2–4 had appeared. Announced in October 1955, outwardly it resembled its predecessor and mechanically the cars differed little, although a minor change was made to the ratio of the rear axle which was 3.77:1 rather than 3.73:1. The top speed, in excess of 115mph (185kph) remained about the same as for the 3-litre-engined DB2–4. Inside there was an improved ventilation system, a new type of fly-off handbrake and better seats. For the first time the two types of body, the mainstream two-door and drophead coupés, were joined by a third, a hard-top or fixed-head coupé version of the design which consequentially was bereft of the distinctive rear opening door.

BROWN BUYS TICKFORD

However, the coachwork was no longer the work of Mulliners of Birmingham but was made by the Tickford body-building concern of Newport Pagnell, which had been an independent company up until December 1954 when it was purchased by David Brown. It was a move of far reaching consequences to Aston Martin, as from 1957 all car production would be transferred to the Buckinghamshire town.

David Brown's purchase of Tickford highlighted the acute shortage of body-building facilities that was plaguing the rapidly growing British motor industry in the 1950s, a limitation which afflicted the 'Big Batallions' and specialist manufacturers alike. Brown's action represented the final link in a chain of events that had begun back in 1953. It was in that year that Ford bought the American-owned Briggs Motor Bodies which had been established alongside its Dagenham factory. The move had been prompted because Ford's managing director, Sir Patrick Hennessy, feared that across the Atlantic Walter Briggs, the firm's founder, would die and its Detroit factory would be bought by Chrysler, its largest customers. If that had happened, a rival corporation would then have controlled the body supply of Ford's British subsidiary. Between 1951 and 1953 he therefore made numerous attempts to buy Briggs' British business and the deal was finally agreed over the telephone in February 1953. The price was $9 million and Ford had to obtain the government's permission to make the purchase in precious dollars. Hennessy would later refer to the Briggs acquisition as the most important event in Ford-Britain's post-war history. As a postscript, it should

be recorded that Hennessy's fears were indeed justified and Chrysler bought Briggs' American operations later in 1953 for $75 million.

Ford's purchase of Briggs was to have a knock-on effect because, six months later, the newly formed British Motor Corporation (as the combined Austin and Morris concerns had become in 1952) followed suit and, in August 1953, announced that it had bought Fisher and Ludlow of Birmingham which built many of its bodies. One of that firm's customers was the Standard Motor Company of Coventry, and BMC's Leonard Lord wasted little time in informing Standard's newly appointed managing director, Alick Dick, that once existing contracts had been seen through Fisher and Ludlow's plant at Tile Hill, Coventry would no longer produce its bodies.

THE MULLINER FACTOR

It will be recalled that some of Standard's work was undertaken by Mulliners Ltd of Birmingham which also built bodies for a number of other smaller car makers, one of which was Aston Martin. With Fisher and Ludlow no longer prepared to make its hulls, Alick Dick turned to Mulliners and, in June 1954, succeeded in obtaining an undertaking from the firm that for a ten-year period it would place its entire body output at Standard's disposal. It was a liaison which would finally be underpinned in 1958 when what had become Standard Triumph purchased the Birmingham company.

Dick's initiative caused problems of varying severity for Alvis, Daimler and Aston Martin, all of which were threatened with the loss of their body manufacturing facility. For Alvis, with burgeoning sales of military vehicles and aero engines, this decision virtually spelt the end of the Alvis car in its current state, although the 3-litre model was revived in Graber-styled form in 1955. BSA, which owned the Daimler company, wasted little time in purchasing Carbodies of Coventry in June 1954. Faced with this predicament, David Brown looked around for an independent coach builder to buy. There were not many of any reasonable size, apart from Tickford Ltd of Newport Pagnell, Buckinghamshire. Like many of its contemporaries, it had nineteenth-century roots and, as Salmons and Sons, had built coaches and open horse-drawn carriages.

FROM SALMONS TO TICKFORD

With the coming of the automobile at the turn of the century, Salmons switched to car bodies. The Tickford name had become current in the 1920s as a body style and the company's title changed to this in 1942 when it was bought by Ian Irvine Boswell, a wealthy car enthusiast from Crawley, Sussex. After the war Tickford had received a Ministry of Supply contract to convert wartime vehicles for civilian use, and had then built estate car bodies on Daimler and Humber chassis. It specialized in drophead coupés and produced these for Alvis, first for the TA14 and then for its Grey Lady and TC21/100 models, and for Healey — it had also created the prototype Healey 100 sports car. Aston Martin already had connections with the firm. It is thought that Tickford assembled fifty-seven of the 359 saloon bodies for the Lagonda saloon which had first appeared in 1948, and was responsible for the 3-litre Mark II saloon, although there were only a mere ten of these produced between September 1952 and July 1953.

The Tickford business consisted of the Newport Pagnell works and a London-based garage which also served as the firm's head office. Boswell retained the latter, based at 6–9 Upper St Martin's Lane, but changed its name from Tickford to Salmons Garages. Once within the ownership of the David

Brown Corporation, Tickford first produced bodies for the DB2–4, prior to the arrival of the Mark II version in the autumn of 1955.

With the introduction of the Mark II, and against a background of a strike-prone bodyshop and deteriorating finances, David Brown took the opportunity of moving the model's assembly from Feltham over 190 miles (305km) north, to Meltham in Yorkshire. It was there that David Brown tractors were manufactured at a former cotton mill bought by the Corporation in 1939. Although this transfer of manufacture resulted in some contraction of the firm's Feltham presence, the Aston Martin and Lagonda drawing office remained there, along with the racing and servicing departments.

THE TOURING CONNECTION

In October 1956, Aston Martin announced that it was ceasing production of its drophead and fixed-head coupés. Demand had been very low and was to stand at twenty-four and thirty-four examples respectively.

At the same time, a new export Aston Martin was announced. It will be recalled that the lines of the Mark II DB2–4 were essentially those of its DB2 predecessor and the new model had a visually adventurous, Italian-styled and built open two-seater body. Called the Superleggera Spyder, it was the work of the celebrated Touring company of Milan. *Superleggera* means 'very light' in Italian and was the name given by Touring to its unique method of body construction. This consisted of a network of small diameter steel tubes, covered by a delicate alloy skin – a strong, rigid but light body resulted. The car sold for £2,500, which was £500 more than the mainstream Mark II and, in truth, it was a flop. Only about three examples were made. Yet when viewed in the light of future events, it represented the first contacts between Aston Martin and

---

Carrozzeria Touring

An essential ingredient in the success of the DB4 and its derivatives was the magnificent lines of its bodywork. On general manager John Wyer's insistence, the styling had to be Italian and was the work of Touring, one of the greatest of the Italian *carrozzerias*.

The firm was established in Milan by Felice Bianchi Anderloni, a former law student who had subsequently worked for Isotta Fraschini. He was joined by Gaetano Ponzoni, a lawyer friend and, late in 1925, they took a controlling interest in the small Falco coach-building concern and changed its name to the English-sounding one of Touring. Anderloni was responsible for the styling and, in the inter-war years, he produced a range of coachwork of unrivalled line and proportion. In view of its Milan location, the firm developed a close relationship with Alfa Romeo which endured until the 1950s. In 1937 Touring perfected a new form of body construction to which it applied the name *Superleggera*, meaning 'very light' in Italian. This consisted of a latticework of load-bearing tubes to which aluminium body panels were attached, resulting in a light, rigid structure. It was a recognition of Anderloni's dictum that 'weight is the enemy and aerodynamic drag the obstacle'.

After the Second World War a new creative team took over. Anderloni had died suddenly in 1948 and his son, Carlo Felice Bianchi Anderloni took his place along with Frederico Formenti. The latter was responsible for styling the Aston Martin DB4. Touring maintained its contacts with Alfa Romeo, the outcome being bodies on the 1900 Sprint and Super Sprint coupés of the 1950s, together with the Pegaso Z102, Lancia Flaminia, Maserati 3500 and Lamborghini 350 GTs.

Regrettably, a combination of lack of orders from a large manufacturer and its own labour troubles resulted in the famous company finally closing its doors in 1967. Recently, however, there has been news of a revival.

Touring, a liaison that would flower gloriously in 1958 when the DB4 would be unveiled, styled by Touring and with its body built in accordance with its Superleggera principles.

The Aston Martin Superleggera Spyder of 1956 had its origins in the previous year when, as a speculative venture, Touring purchased a left-hand drive DB2–4 Mark II chassis and proceeded to design a body for it. Drawings had been completed by December 1955 and were the work of Touring's talented stylist, Frederico Formenti. The competence and individuality of its low, purposeful lines underlined all the vigour of Italian styling, and perhaps the only unhappy aspect of the design was the presence of angular dummy air vents just behind either door.

The car first appeared at the Turin Motor Show in April 1956 and the idea was subsequently taken up by Aston Martin, with at least two further cars being built. One appeared at the 1956 Paris Motor Show and another at the London one. There *The Motor* declared that its 'sheer beauty . . . would be hard to surpass . . . and is undoubtedly the high spot of this year's Motor Show'. Its presence underlined the massive gulf that existed between Italian stylists and their British counterparts, a state of affairs that was highlighted by the fact that the Touring body and the all too traditional Mark II DB2–4 drophead coupé were contemporaries. It was a disparity that would not be lost on Aston Martin's general manager, John Wyer.

COMPETITION SUCCESS

Under the bonnet of the Superleggera Spyder was an uprated version of the 3-litre Lagonda engine. This was fitted as standard on the export cars and was available on those on sale in Britain at extra cost.

*The starting point of Aston Martin's associations with Carrozzeria Touring
began in 1956 when the Milan styling house bodied this left-hand drive DB2–4.
It is pictured at that year's Paris Motor Show.*

Essentially it consisted of a new cylinder head with high-lift camshafts, larger valves and a twin exhaust system, ministrations which resulted in a rise of output from 140bhp to 165bhp. It would have given the already lightened car a top speed well in excess of 120mph (193kph).

The London show car came to national prominence when it was offered as the prize in a competition staged by the *Daily Mail*. The contest was won by Alexander Smith, an apprentice joiner from Crail, Fifeshire, who was judged to have submitted the best slogan which was: 'Who said a Spyder couldn't fly?' Ironically, he was not a driver and could not take a test though the prize included a contribution of £700 towards running expenses.

The Mark II DB2–4, in production for close on two years between October 1955 and August 1957, was not a success and only 199 were sold. This compared with 565 examples of the original DB2–4 produced over a similar time span. What Aston Martin desperately needed was a replacement for the ageing DB2, the origins of which reached back to the pre-War years. Its absence was the result, in part, of the firm having spent too much of its time and resources on motor racing. In Wyer's words, by 1957:

Aston Martin was in the position of having a product which had largely ceased to appeal to the buying public . . . For the first time since 1950 we were in the position of being able to produce more cars than we could sell.

The versatility of the original DB2 theme was underlined with the arrival of the DB2–4 in 1953 with rear-opening door. This is the DB Mark III which appeared in 1957 and remained in production until 1959, so overlapping the DB4.

The losses were mounting to the point when even David Brown was begining to look at them in askance. It was not a happy time to take on the General Managership.
The Certain Sound, John Wyer (Haynes, 1981).

DARK DAYS

It should be said that there was a time when Aston Martin had been marginally profitable. In 1950 the firm returned a surplus of a mere £107, but this rose to £12,640 in 1953 while 1954's figure slumped to £1,557. There then followed a period of recurring deficits. Against this background, serious consideration was given to closing the business down temporarily, until the arrival of the much needed DB4. But if that had been done, it would have meant that the skilled workforce, on which the firm's prosperity so much

depended, would have been dispersed irrevocably and probably lost for ever.

Before such a drastic course of action was adopted, David Brown and Alan Avison (his deputy managing director, operations) decided that it would be well worth while if John Wyer made a world tour to try and stimulate sufficient overseas orders to keep the firm in business. However, he clearly needed something to sell and so, says Wyer, 'we cobbled together the Mark III'.

In view of John Wyer's overseas sales tour, the Mark III was simultaneously launched at the Geneva Motor Show and in America in March 1957. Not only did it look different from its predecessor but some radical modifications were made to the 3-litre engine. Externally, changes were made to the front of the car with a new, curved radiator grille, echoing that of the DB3S sports racer. This, in turn, reduced the bonnet line which had the effect of making the car appear lower. The work had been undertaken by Donald Hayter, who had joined Aston Martin as a draughtsman in 1954.

MAREK'S MODIFICATIONS

The first significant changes were also made to the Lagonda engine and it was reworked by Aston Martin's new engine designer, Tadek Marek, of whom more anon. The cylinder head, available on the Mark II, was carried over but changes were also made to the block. The crankcase was stiffened up and modifications were also made to the cylinder liners to avoid distortion through the head being over-tightened, a shortcoming that had been experienced in the earlier engines. They were now sealed at the top rather than just at the bottom as had previously been the case. The new liners also benefited from some improved water cooling at the top and, at the lower end, there were two O-rings with leak-off holes in the side of the block to allow any water to escape that had managed to pass the first ring. Minor changes were also made to the design of the crankshaft and it was forged in stronger steel. There was a new oil pump and the chain tensioner was manually adjusted rather than hydraulically as had previously been the case. The clutch was also now hydraulically rather than mechanically operated and provision was made for the fitment of an overdrive unit.

Girling disc brakes, having proved their worth on the DB3S, were available at extra cost and were standardized when the model replaced the Mark II on the British market in October 1957; Alfin drums were fitted at the rear. For a time the car had the desired effect and was to sell far better than its Mark II predecessor, particularly in America, and eventually 551 were built over a two-year period.

By the time that the Mark III entered production in March 1957, the former Tickford works at Newport Pagnell had been completely reorganized, so that as much as possible could be made on the premises and final assembly took place there rather than at Meltham, although Feltham continued as before. In addition to bodywork, engine production was transferred to the Buckinghamshire factory from a David Brown factory at Farsley, Yorkshire but gearbox manufacture continued in the north. There was a fascinating historical parallel to the Tickford works becoming host to a car manufacturer. Back in 1923, Salmons and Sons had produced a Meadows-engined light car, named the N.P. after the town. Only 395 examples had been produced before the Salmons Light Car Company was wound up in 1925.

DB4 PROTOTYPE

While John Wyer had been abroad in the first part of 1957, in an itinerary that embraced Australia, New Zealand, America and Canada, he was left in little doubt by Aston Martin dealers of the urgent need for a DB2 replacement. Fortunately, by July 1957, the prototype of the all-new DB4 had been completed and Wyer would soon be subjecting it to rigorous Continental testing.

In theory, Aston Martin already had a DB4 prototype in the shape of Project 114 completed in 1956 but Wyer, in particular, was not satisfied with the finished product and made the decision that instead of the body being designed at Feltham the work would be entrusted to an Italian stylist. As Harold Beach remembers: 'he wanted something really striking and the finished product certainly bore out the wisdom of that decision'.

British manufacturers had been inspired directly by Italian stylists, particularly in the performance field, since the early 1930s. It was then that examples of the six-cylinder 1750 and eight-cylinder 2300 Alfa Romeo sports cars began to arrive in Britain in appreciable numbers, usually clad with visually impressive open two-seater bodies. These were invariably the work of the Zagato or Touring companies which, like Alfa Romeo, were based in Milan. Their delectable lines were skilfully interpreted by such British car makers as Riley with its Imp, MPH and Sprite models, on William Lyons' SS and on the rare and sleek Squire.

After the Second World War, the Italian styling houses took on an international stature with Pinin Farina, in particular, moving forward to emerge as the best known *carrozzeria* of its day. Yet another factor was that Italy had a new marque in the shape of Ferrari. Its road cars were, in the first instance, mostly fitted with Touring coachwork but, from 1953, Pinin Farina obtained an exclusive contract for Ferrari's body supply. Both firms produced mostly closed, or *Gran Turismo* coachwork but there were also some spyder (open) bodies. Such British sports car as the Austin Healey and AC Ace soon began to echo the lines of the latter.

THE ITALIAN CONNECTION

Farina's influence attracted the attention of the European mass producers (namely Peugeot in France) while the British Motor Corporation, the country's largest car maker, retained the Turin company to style its new range. The first model to benefit from this Italian influence appeared in the A40 of 1958 which was followed by the front-wheel 1100 model of 1962, destined to be the best-selling British car of the decade.

In view of Pinin Farina's pre-eminence, it was perhaps inevitable that Wyer would first approach that company to style the DB4, however, the liaison was not to be.

This was because Farina worked in steel and Aston Martin and Tickford's experience was with aluminium, the material having to be used in the interests of lightness. So the decision was made to go to Touring, the firm that had produced the Superleggera Spyder Mark II DB2–4 in 1956. Harold Beach therefore went to Milan, complete with a set of chassis drawings of the DB4. He recalls that Touring's first response was:

'We can't build a body on this [perimeter] chassis. It's got to have a platform frame so that our Superleggera structure can be fully integrated.' At the time we were in the era of separate bodies and chassis and I didn't really look that far ahead.'

On his return to Feltham, Beach says: 'I told John Wyer what Touring had said and he wanted to know how long it would take to design a new platform frame. I told him six weeks.' This was duly accomplished and Beach was able to study the platform of the Alfa Romeo 1900 Sprint that Touring had produced in small numbers between 1951 and 1958.

THE MILAN MAESTROS

The platform chassis was shipped to Italy and a drawing, produced by Don Hayter, was sent to Touring showing the lines of the sort of body Aston Martin had in mind. Hayter had left Feltham early in 1956 and joined MG where he was later responsible for styling the long-running MGB sports car.

At Touring, the DB4's body was the work of Frederico Formenti, who had been responsible for the 1956 Superleggera Spyder. He differed from his British counterparts in that he was also a skilled model maker and would be responsible for the 1:10 epowood model of the design. At Feltham, as with other British car makers, such work was invariably assigned to two individuals.

There Frank Feeley's sketches were skilfully interpreted by the firm's resident model maker, Ernie Game.

While Touring was producing the first DB4 body, the new car's engine was in a well-advanced state. John Wyer had been the first to recognize that the days of the Bentley-designed Lagonda unit were numbered and had decided therefore that the DB4 would require a completely new power unit. David Brown recounted in *The Power Behind Aston Martin*, Geoff Courtney (Oxford Illustrated Press, 1978) that discussions went on into many a night as to just what form the replacement engine should take:

We had a V12 Lagonda engine . . . [but] had constant crankshaft failures . . . and there was a lot of heart searching as to whether we should try to rectify the errors and make this the replacement. We also did quite a lot of talking around the possibility of a V8 but eventually we opted for a six-cylinder.

This was the work of Aston Martin's new engine designer, Tadek Marek, a Pole who had arrived in England in 1941 and, during the war, had been involved with tank design. In 1949 he moved to the motor industry, which was his first love, and he obtained a job with Austin at its Longbridge factory. One of his assignments (but which never reached production) was to create an experimental V8 engine incorporating A40 parts.

A NEW ENGINEER

Marek found the economic constraints at Austin frustrating, however, and after two years he returned to work on tanks and was

---

Tadek Marek (1908–1982)

The designer of the six-cylinder twin overhead camshaft engine that powered the DB4, DB5 and DB6 was Polish and was born in the city of Krakow. Marek received his seven-year technical education in Germany at the prestigious Charlottenburg Technical Institute in Berlin. He soon developed a passion for motor racing and, in 1928, was competing at the city's Avus circuit when the car in front of him skidded and he shot over the top of the banking and into a marquee. Later, he would delight in recounting this story because he believed that he held the world record for demolishing soda siphons, the tent having contained around 500 of them! He did, however, sustain serious injuries which included the loss of a kidney. Despite his racing career being at an end, Marek continued to participate in rallies and trials. By the late 1930s he was working for Fiat's and then General Motors' Polish subsidiaries. The outbreak of the Second World war in 1939 produced its inevitable upheavals and, after an incident filled three years, Marek finally arrived in Britain in 1941. He joined the Polish Army, but his engineering training saw him back at his drawing board designing tanks. After the war Tadek spent some time in Germany with the United Nations Relief and Rehabilitation Association to assist in post-war reconstruction, but he returned to Britain in 1949 and joined Austin which was to lead to him arriving at Aston Martin in 1954.

A very fast though safe driver with a highly individual style, at Feltham he ran a 3-litre engined DB2 with a 5-speed Maserati gearbox and later had a lightened left-hand drive DB4 from France, the engine of which had suffered from the crankshaft bearing failure that plagued the early cars. He duly rebuilt it with a 4-litre Vantage engine. A controversial figure, he produced both love and hatred from his colleagues in about equal proportions! His great redeeming feature was his humour and one of his contemporaries, Mike Loasby, has remembered him as having 'a superb, dry sense of humour. A bounder with twinkling eyes.'

After he left Aston Martin in 1968, Marek and his wife lived in Italy for a time, but returned to Britain and the Hampshire village of Selbourne where he died in 1982.

involved in the creation of the amphibious version of the famous Centurion. In late 1953 he applied for a job with Aston Martin, and was interviewed by the manager, James Stirling, who intimated that the job was his. He and his wife then went off for a Sicilian holiday but, awaiting them on their return, was a letter stating that the job was not available after all. At this point, Marek wasted little time in presenting himself at the David Brown Corporation's Huddersfield headquarters to demand an explanation. It then emerged that the letter had been sent as the result of an administrative error and Tadek Marek joined Aston Martin in 1954. His first assignment was to undertake the modifications that appeared in the Mark III in 1957, but from thereon Marek was solely concerned with the design of the new engine for the DB4.

When he and Aston Martin's general manager first spoke about the new engine, John Wyer has said that Marek:

Made two stipulations. One was that he would design the cylinder block in cast iron which was where all his experience lay. I agreed to this, but reluctantly, because I was very concerned about weight. The second was that I would not use his engine for racing, because, as he said, he had no experience of designing racing engines. I gave him a conditional promise that I would not do so without consulting him and would give weight to his views.

As it transpired John Wyer would have to break his promises although, as it will emerge, this was for reasons completely beyond his control.

ORIGINALLY IRON

The long-running discussions between David Brown, John Wyer and Tadek Marek had resulted in the decision to perpetuate the concept of a six-cylinder twin overhead cam-shaft unit, as exemplified by the current Lagonda engine. Tadek therefore began work on the design in 1955 and, armed with these preliminary drawings, he and Wyer sought out the Midland Motor Cylinder Company at its stand at that year's motor show. However, the Aston Martin men were in for a shock because, according to Wyer, 'they received us with a certain amount of hilarity and told us that they had no spare capacity in their iron foundry for at least 18 months'. Wyer's and Marek's pleas were to no avail but the firm did point out that, if the engine was redesigned in aluminium, the work could then be undertaken swiftly by MMC's associate company, Birmingham Alumin-ium, which had spare capacity and was look-ing for work. In view of the all-important time factor, Wyer had little choice than to accept this radical change to the design of the DB4's engine. As he has since pointed out, the car ended up with an aluminium cylinder block almost by accident. However, Wyer has also reflected candidly that:

The DB4 would have been a better produc-tion engine had we been able to follow Marek's original concept. With an alumin-ium block, it has always been compared unfavourably, in terms of smoothness and silence, with its counterpart, the Jaguar.

Conversely, it did give Aston Martin the basis of a racing unit though, in doing so, Marek's second stipulation was broken. His original brief had been to produce a 3-litre unit. This was because as Wyer said in 'The Development of the DB4', circa 1959; repro-duced in *AM Magazine*, Spring, 1990:

We believed that a sports car, such as the Aston Martin, should be 3 litre capacity. This thought was influenced by the demands of racing, which had always been the cornerstone of our engineering policy, and it is interesting that the 3 litre limit for International Sports car events was not adopted by the F.I.A. until 1958. For the Lagonda, with increased weight and the probable demands of automatic transmission, it was thought that a larger engine than 3 litres might be required.

TWO OUT OF ONE

It was estimated that the greatest possible capacity range that could be embodied by one design was about 750cc. The 3-litre engine would be a 92 × 75mm unit which would give 2,992cc while the Lagonda version would be a 'square' 92 × 92mm one, giving a capacity of 3,670cc. Because the firm already had a sound 3-litre engine in the Bentley-designed unit, Marek began work on the larger capacity one in the first week of August 1955, designated DP 186, which perpetuated the concept of the existing twin overhead camshaft six.

In retrospect, Wyer considered that their thinking had been based on a false premise. He subsequently recognized that an engine's size was not dictated by its bore and stroke but by the dimensions of the main bearings, which governed the length of the crankshaft and so the engine's overall dimensions. As a result, he continues:

[Marek] very correctly made the bearings adequate for the larger version; because he is also cautious he made them generous . . . The result was a design which, from the start, was too big to be a 3 litre. On the other hand it was found possible to increase the size of this engine to 4.2 litres with complete reliability . . . It would seem therefore, that our original estimate of 750cc as the 'bracket' which could be covered by one basic design was not far wrong. The argument was sound, but we started from the wrong end.

So the DB4 ended up with the engine originally intended for the Lagonda saloon! The 3.7-litre unit ran for the first time on the test bench in November 1956. It had been designed to produce 180bhp and Wyer was delighted that 'this the engine achieved the very first time it ran, in my experience an almost unprecedented performance for an entirely new design'. The engine was also built in 95 × 92mm 4-litre dimensions. All these engines were briefly used as alternative power units in Aston Martin's new generation of sports racing cars.

THE CUTTING EDGE

It will be remembered that, back in 1955, Ted Cutting had begun work on Aston Martin's all-new DBR1 sports racer. This used a spaceframe chassis, although Cutting retained the DB3S's trailing arm independent front suspension, a Watts linkage was employed in conjunction with the de Dion rear axle, the gearbox was moved and the five-speed David Brown unit was incorporated in the final drive.

The heart of the car was the new dry-sump alloy RB6 six-cylinder twin overhead camshaft engine. In its 3-litre form, it retained the 83 × 90mm dimensions of the LG6, but Cutting dispensed with the unnecessarily elaborate and troublesome 'cheeses'. These were replaced by a conventional seven main bearing layout which required the creation of a new crankshaft and meant that the connecting rods were also redesigned. By perpetuating the same cylinder centres as the Lagonda engine, the twin overhead camshaft and twin-plug cylinder head (with a 60-degree valve angle) were carried over from its predecessor.

This arrangement survived until 1957 when a new '95-degree head' which permitted larger valves was phased in. In 1958 the bore size was upped to 84mm, so breaking any links with the previous unit. As Frank Feeley had left Feltham by this time, the hard-working and versatile Ted Cutting was also responsible for the lines of its impressive open two-seater body.

The DBR1 made its first appearance running as a prototype in 2½-litre form at Le Mans in 1956, although as a weakened mixture was used to conserve fuel, it ran its bearings after twenty hours while lying in seventh position. Aston Martin spirits rose when a DB3S, driven by Stirling Moss and Peter Collins, was placed second even though for the second consecutive year this was behind a D-type Jaguar. Despite this success, 1956 represented the DB3S's swan-song. From then on all hopes would be pinned on the DBR1.

The following year of 1957 was one of varying fortunes. The DBR1 ran for the first time at Spa in 3-litre form and examples came in first and second. Despite this success, Tony Brooks in the winning car experienced a problem when he came to change down from fourth to third gear. Although he went on to win, the lever had jammed in fourth. It was a malady that was to plague the car with varying degrees of severity during that season and the following one. At Nurburgring, the DBR1 gave Aston Martin its first victory in the 1,000-Kilometre Race.

AN OPPORTUNITY MISSED

Fortunately at Le Mans, the previous year's capacity limit had been dispensed with. Aston Martin entered two DBR1s but, to save building a third car the DBR2 was created, powered by Tadek Marek's new 3.7-litre twin cam six, destined for the DB4. This was united with the Project 166 Lagonda spaceframe and cloaked in a rather DBR1-like body. It was ready in time for the race but, as it was an unproven car, the best drivers had been allotted the DBR1. The driving was shared by two brothers, Peter and Graham Whitehead. The DBR2 proved to be very fast in practice but the car dropped out after only seven laps. Its gearbox had failed as the result of a blocked breather and had pumped out all its lubricant.

In John Wyer's opinion the DBR2 could have been capable of winning Le Mans that year but was the victim of a stupid mistake. It had been bench-tested at Feltham with six Weber 48 DCOE carburettors but, when the unit was installed in the car, modifications had to be made to the somewhat elaborate fuel delivery system. Once back at the factory, it was discovered that these changes had caused misfiring and fuel starvation over 5,000rpm. With the layout used in the race it returned 230bhp, which was a loss of more than 50bhp, but even in that state it had lapped at 4 minutes 16 seconds. By this miscalculation, Aston Martin lost the publicity it would have received if the new engine, destined for its new road car, had won Le Mans first time out.

The two DBR1s were equally unlucky. Both failed to finish having stuck in fourth gear and had to withdraw, a calamity which can hardly have done much for the international reputation of David Brown Gears.

In 1958 came a change in racing regulations. World Sports Car Championship events would be run with 3-litre capacity which was ideal for the DBR1. For non-Championship events in Britain, the factory fielded the DBR2, running for the first time in 4-litre form, with some success. Stirling Moss won the sports car race in the Easter Goodwood meeting and he was also victorious in the British Empire Trophy at Oulton Park with Tony Brooks second in another example. The May Silverstone meeting was less successful and Lister-Jaguars dominated the field, although Salvadori and Brooks came in fourth and fifth. Stirling Moss took the wheel of the DBR3 which was essentially a DBR1 with the DB4 engine prepared in short-stroke 3-litre state. In the event it ran its bearings and the concept was not pursued.

A revival in Aston Martin's sports racing fortunes began in 1957 with the arrival of the Ted Cutting designed DBR1. The occasion is the 1958 Tourist Trophy race at Goodwood with, left to right, the cars of Stirling Moss/Tony Brooks, Roy Salvadori/Jack Brabham and Caroll Shelby/Stuart Lewis-Evans. The event was an Aston Martin hat trick with Moss first, Salvadori second and Shelby third.

TRANSAXLE TROUBLES

Le Mans once again proved a disappointment and all three DBR1s failed to finish; Moss's engine blew up while he was comfortably in the lead, the second car crashed and the third dropped out, once again with transaxle problems. Nevertheless the Whitehead brothers, driving a privately entered DB3S, were second behind a Ferrari.

But it had not been all gloom. Moss had scored a celebrated victory for the second year running in the Nurburgring 1,000-Kilometre Race and, in September, the cars easily won the shortened Tourist Trophy race, with DBR1s also coming in second and third.

On 1 October 1958, just two and a half weeks following this triumph at Goodwood, came the announcement of the DB4, a mere fifteen months after the completion of the first prototype designated DP 184/1. Sprayed blue with matching upholstery, it had arrived at Feltham in the summer of 1957 though it was minus its engine, gearbox and transmission. It was then a matter of working day and night to fit these components and the car was completed late on a Saturday afternoon in July 1957. Beach thinks that he was the first person to drive it: 'I took it down to the Chertsey roundabout, which was our unofficial test run, and it seemed pretty good.' But what next? Both

David Brown and John Wyer were out of the country but were due to return on the following day. Knowing Wyer as he did, Harold was certain he would telephone him at home to find out how the prototype performed. So he took the car home, parked it in his drive and 'sure enough Wyer phoned later that night wanting to know how we'd got on. "What you've got to do", he said, "is to take it down to David Brown's place [Chequers Farm, Fulmer, Buckinghamshire] tomorrow." '

A PROMISING START

Wyer arrived at Beach's house on the following morning and they then drove to Brown's farm. 'David Brown was a magnificent driver and we tore all over the Chilterns with Wyer in the front and me, crouched in the back'. On their return, David Brown turned to Harold and said: 'this is a very promising motor car.'

The next thing was to give the prototype a really long Continental run and this is what Wyer did, in August and September 1957. When he left, there were 2,500 miles (4,023km) on the car's speedometer and he put on a further 2,000 miles (3,219km). On his return to Feltham, Wyer wrote a comprehensive report on the car's performance and concluded his description thus:

While there remains a considerable amount of development work to be carried out, it is not too early to say that we have a car that can justly be described as 'Grand Touring'. The overall impression at the end of this test is that the car has magnificent performance and is full of promise. While faults were fairly numerous, as was to be expected, they were not fundamental and should not be too difficult to eradicate.

Not that the trip had been without incident. Wyer elected to take his wife on the journey and had decided to return the car to Touring in Milan for discussion and comment. Unfortunately, while in France and crossing the Vosges, the Aston Martin's brake pedal progressively began to lose its effect, until the prototype was virtually brakeless. Wyer said nothing to his wife, although she clearly noticed that something was amiss when they reached the Swiss frontier at Basle and the car slid under the stripped customs pole which nearly hit the windscreen. The brakes were then bled, but they soon began to deteriorate again and virtually disappeared by the time that Wyer reached the base of the St Gothard Pass. Whereas the ascent might have been manageable, he decided to put the DB4 on the train at Goschenen and dispatched it to Airolo. This still left the 22-mile (37km) descent into Biasca. From there on it was a matter of using low gears all the way and the rather inadequate handbrake. Como, just over the Italian border, was reached without incident and the last few kilometres along the autoroute were covered safely, although Wyer entered Milan feeling that he had aged several years!

DE DION DELETED

Perhaps the most serious shortcoming that had emerged during the testing was the noise which emanated from the spiral bevel, rather than the hypoid, final drive unit. It will be recalled that Beach had specified a de Dion rear axle and its 3.27:1 differential was mounted directly on the chassis. Wyer considered this too high and recommended that the production DB4 was fitted with a 3.54:1 ratio, the production car being so equipped.

However, the problem of the noisy differential remained. To quote Beach:

The problem was that we couldn't find a suitable chassis mounted drive unit. At the time, Jaguar hadn't yet gone independent, [it would not do so until 1961] so we couldn't go to Salisbury Transmissions and get one for our de Dion. So the only thing was to go to David Brown Gears and get them to make us one. This they did but it was unacceptably noisy so the only thing was to forget about the de Dion axle and fit a live Salisbury axle instead.

Making such a change presented further problems because it meant redesigning the frame, yet again. Touring then built a second green-finished prototype (DP 184/2) and this was duly fitted with the live rear axle. After assembly at Feltham, it was dispatched to Newport Pagnell for members of the workforce to acquaint themselves thoroughly with the car and also get to know the Superleggera method of construction. As it was an integral part of the body structure, Aston Martin was to manufacture the system under licence.

Although much of the firm's resources had been expended on the DB4, the current DB Mark III was not overlooked and improvements were made to that car for the 1959 model year because, incredible as it might seem, there were fears that the DB4 might flop.

MORE POWER

Changes to the engine, borne of racing experience, were made. In its standard twin SU carburettored 162bhp form, the Lagonda six, with an 8.16:1 compression ratio, was designated the DBA unit. A 180bhp special series DBD version was announced as an option in the Mark III, fitted with twin or triple SU carburettors. Top of the range was the 195bhp DBB series, with 8.68:1 compression ratio, and three twin choke Weber 35 DCO carburettors or a similar number of SUs. This engine was only specified with a twin exhaust system. There was also, theoretically, the highly tuned DBC unit which gave 214bhp, but only one car was so equipped.

Improvements were also made to the braking system with the introduction of a Baldwin hydro-boaster servo unit which eased the excessive pedal pressure created by the fitting of front disc brakes.

Aston Martin did not need to have any fears about the success of the DB4. The Mark III only remained in production until July 1959 because the new car received a rapturous reception when it made its débuts at the 1958 Paris and London Motor Shows.

3 DB4: Right but not Ready

'The DB4 is more powerful than any touring car hitherto marketed by a British factory, and will probably prove to be the fastest.'
The Motor, 1 October 1958.

With the Aston Martin DB4's top speed approaching the 140mph (225kph) mark, it was not only the quickest car in Britain but also one of the fastest four-seaters in the world, putting it on a par with the best of the Italian *Gran Turismos*.

Not only that, the DB4 looked sensational. Its lines had been so superbly executed by Touring that it stood head and shoulders above practically all of its contemporaries in the performance car field and triumphantly vindicated John Wyer's decision to have had this latest Aston Martin styled in Italy. It was also completely new with nothing carried over from previous models. At £3,976, it was the most expensive Aston Martin ever built and was close on a £1,000 more than the DB Mark III that it was to replace. For that price, you could have bought two Jaguar XK150 coupés at £1,763 apiece, though it was still about £500 less than Britain's other mainline Grand Tourer, the hand-built Bristol 406.

The car was unveiled at the Paris Motor Show which opened for ten days on 2 October, and the single pale-primrose example shared the Aston Martin stand with a Mark III car. John Wyer was naturally present for the launch and has recalled that Marcel Blondeau, the firm's French distributor, came up, tears in his eyes, and told him, 'This is not a car, it is a folly, but I can sell as many as you can supply.'

Later, over lunch with David Brown at Fouquets in the Champs-Elysées, Wyer remembered that 'he gave me his warm congratulations, which meant more to me than all the plaudits of the press and the public.'

At this time there was only one car available for demonstration purposes. After the Paris Show which closed on 12 October, the precious primrose DB4 was transported to London to take pride of place on the Aston Martin stand at the London Motor Show which opened at Earls Court on 22 October. It went without saying that the new car was the star of the 1958 London Motor Show, *The Motor* reported that 'The new DB4 . . . painted in pale primrose, dominated not only the Aston Martin stand but the show itself.' These sentiments were shared by its weekly rival *The Autocar* which remarked: 'One of the most inspiring specialist sports cars to be shown in London for some time is the new Aston Martin DB4 . . . [it] is probably the fastest four seater production car in the world today.'

At the London event, Wyer was greeted by an enthusiastic Kjell Quave, who sold Aston Martins in San Francisco, with the news that he would order 1,000 cars if the factory could undertake to deliver them. When Wyer informed him that, even on their most optimistic projection, they planned to produce no more than half that number, he responded with, 'Well, I will take all you can build.'

This is the moment to take a closer look at

The DB4, as it originally appeared in October 1958. One of the fastest Grand Tourers of its day, it was also the most expensive Aston Martin ever, selling at £3,976.

the car that John Wyer, Harold Beach, Tadek Marek and the team at Feltham had created. Like its DB2 predecessor, the DB4 was a two-door coupé and although it was a four-seater, in truth, only children could be carried in any comfort.

SUPERLEGGERA BODY

Consisting entirely of aluminium, the body was built in accordance with Touring's Superleggera principles and was therefore mounted on a trellis of small-diameter steel tubes welded together. The body panels were attached to this structure and clinched around angle plates which were welded to

the members, with graphite pads sandwiched between the two. Such items as the windscreen, rear window frames and angle sections for the door hinges were attached directly to the frame.

The windscreen had a pronounced rake and the slim proportions of the pillars resulted in excellent all-round visibility. The roof swept into the tail in a single and subtly tapering line, and skilfully merged into the boot lid. This was a well-established feature of Touring bodies and had figured on many of the exquisite Berlinettas that the firm had produced for Alfa Romeo when it first introduced its Superleggera body in 1937.

This body structure was, in turn, mounted on a platform chassis. One of the advantages

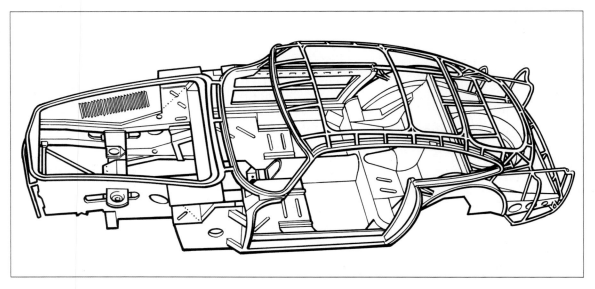

The DB4 and DB5 shared essentially the same Superleggera body constrsuction.

of such a design was that a low seating position could be achieved without the use of deep sills. There were sills, however, and these formed the main side members. About mid-way along the door openings was a substantial box section cross member which ran across the car and was around half the depth of the sills.

The floor panels were an integral part of the structure, along with the scuttle, rear seat pan and wing arches. Ahead of the scuttle there were box sections on either side which terminated in a similar transverse cross member to which the front suspension was attached. There was also a vertical member at this point which was braced into the forward facing arms, and these combined to form the front wing valances.

BETTER SEATING

The doors, which undercut the wrap-around windscreen, were wide, their windows frameless and they sealed against rubber mouldings on the body. Unlike the DB2–4, the DB4 was not fitted with quarter lights. The rear windows also opened and hinged along their forward edges. Entry to the rear seats was easy because the backs of the front ones hinged forward to give access to them. These were adjustable Reutter units, but the rear seat was a full width one with the intrusive propeller shaft tunnel in between the two squabs. This was a great improvement on the rather rudimentary rear seats provided in the DB2–4, which were known as 'lavatory seats' at the works. The finest quality Connolly hides were also used for the trimming.

Instrumentation was similar to that of the Mark III, and it had a black, leather-covered fascia; there was also a handsome 16in (41cm) wood-rimmed steering wheel. The column itself had two positions for fore and aft movement and the angle was also adjustable.

The rear window was rather more of a roof light. Directly below it, inside the car, was a wide parcel shelf which concealed the presence of a 19-gallon (86-litre) petrol tank. At the back of the car the boot lid opened to floor level and the battery, which had its own master switch, was placed behind a panel in the right-hand wing. Its opposite number was used for stowing the tool kit while the spare wheel was carried in a separate container under the boot floor. So much for the body, but what of the mechanicals?

ALUMINIUM ENGINE

Under the rear opening bonnet, which incorporated a large air intake, was Tadek Marek's new 3,670cc twin overhead camshaft six-cylinder engine. On right-hand drive cars this was offset to the left and, on left-hand drive ones, the opposite applied. As already indicated, it was an aluminium unit with the cylinder head and the block/crankcase made of this material. Marek was later to recognize that when the decision was made to use aluminium:

I was a bit taken aback because I had never seen an aluminium engine working well before – certainly I had never designed one. Ted Cutting [with the RB6 engine] was not in a much better position either, but we decided to go ahead. As it turned out it was the right thing to do.

'Aluminium A.M. Engines', Tadek Marek, *AM Magazine*, 10 (28).

Undoubtedly, the main advantage was that of weight saving. With ancillaries, the cast-iron Lagonda engine weighed 614lb (278kg) and the DB4 was a substantial 48lb (22kg) less at 566lb (257kg).

As far as the cylinder head was concerned, the twin overhead camshafts operated the valves directly through inverted steel tappets. Unlike the Jaguar XK engine, which used shims to achieve the correct clearance, no such arrangement was used by Aston Martin and the clearance was obtained by

grinding the end of the valve stem. The valves were splayed at an angle of 80 degrees, the seats all had inserts and the exhaust guides were in direct contact with the cooling water. The combustion chambers were hemispherical and fully machined. The camshafts themselves were chain driven in two stages from the crankshaft with two Duplex chains which met at a half-speed idler gear. Adjustment was by manually operated jockey sprockets because the automatic variety was thought to be unreliable when fitted to high-performance engines. The distributor, driven by skew-gears, was situated at right angles from the inlet camshaft and was readily accessible for adjustment. There was a single KLG sparking plug per cylinder. The twin 2in (50.8mm) SU HD8 carburettors were mounted on the right-hand side of the engine and fed through two separate three-branch inlet manifolds. The twin exhaust pipes, which ran into a common silencer, was standardized.

The block followed the contours of the liners which combined to save weight and strengthen the structure. Chrome vanadium wet cylinder liners were located by a flange at their upper ends, and at their base, Marek perpetuated the sealing system that he had introduced in the DB2–4 Mark III engine with the use of two O-rings and crankcase-located weep holes.

INTERNAL ARRANGEMENTS

The crankshaft was a massive, nitrided steel forging which ran in seven steel-back, lead bronze 2¾in (70mm) diameter bearings. Like Ted Cutting, Tadek Marek made no attempt to perpetuate the 'cheeses' of the Lagonda engine. The connecting rods were

(Overleaf) *The side view of the 1963 DB4. The duct in the front wing allowed hot air to escape from the engine compartment.*

3.7-LITRE DB4 AND 4-LITRE DB5

Production	1958–1963 3.7-litre	1963–1965 4-litre
Engine		
Block material	Aluminium alloy	
Head material	Aluminium alloy	
Cylinders	In-line six	
Cooling	Water	
Bore and stroke	92 × 92mm	96 × 92mm
Capacity	3,670cc	3,995cc
Main Bearings	7	
Valves	2 per cylinder, dohc	
Compression Ratio	8.2:1	8.8:1
Vantage	9.1	
Carburettors	Twin SU HD8	Triple SU HD8
Vantage	Triple SU HD8	Triple Weber
Max Power (net)*	240bhp @ 5,500rpm	282bhp @ 5,500rpm
Vantage	266bhp @ 5,750rpm	314bhp @ 5,750rpm
Max torque	240lb ft @ 4,250rpm	288lb ft @ 3,850rpm
Transmission		
Clutch	Single dry plate	Twin plate diaphragm
Type	Four speed, synchromesh on all gears	Five speed, synchromesh on all gears
Gear Ratios		
Top		3.14
4th	3.54	3.77
3rd	4.42	4.64
2nd	6.16	6.64
1st	8.82	10.18
Reverse	8.58	12.5
Final Drive	3.54	3.31
Suspension and Steering		
Front	Independent, wishbones and coil springs	
Rear	Live axle, trailing links, Watts linkage, coils springs	
Steering	Rack and pinion	
Tyres	6.00–16	6.70–15
Wheels	Dunlop centre lock	
Rim size	5.5in	
Brakes		
Type	Dunlop disc with Lockheed vacuum servo assistance	Girling disc with separate servos
Size	Front: 11.5in, Rear: 11.125in	Front: 11.5in, Rear: 10.8in

Dimensions		
Wheelbase	98in (2,489mm)	
Track	Front: 54in (1,372mm), Rear 53.5in (1,358mm)	
Overall length	176.375in (4,480mm)	180in (4,572mm)
Overall width	66in (1,676mm)	
Overall height	51.5in (1,308mm)	53in (1,346mm)
Ground clearance	7in (177mm)	6.3in (160mm)
Unladen weight	25.7cwt (1,311kg)	28.8cwt (1,465kg)

*For actual figures, *see* this page (DB4), page 80 (Vantage) and page 110 (DB5).

polished all over and weight graded while the pistons had two compression rings, the top one being chromium faced. Thereafter came a single twin segment oil control ring. All were above the fully floating gudgeon pin secured by circlips.

The Hobourn Eaton oil pump was mounted externally on the right-hand side of the engine. Driven from the crankshaft by a chain, this, by contrast, had a hydraulic chain tensioner. There was a light alloy sump containing 15pt (8.5 litres) of lubricant which circulated via a full-flow Purolator oil filter.

On the model's announcement, this engine was said to have developed 263bhp gross and 240bhp net. In fact, the 3.7-litre twin cam six developed somewhat less than that – in truth, 208bhp. As Marek was to recall, John Wyer asked him:

'What will be done to bring our power advertisements in line with the others?' I said, 'I'll give you the answer tomorrow'. I looked up all the American engines taking the gross horsepower and the net horsepower, added them together and took the mean. It came to 32 per cent above. John Wyer said, 'We can't lie that much, we can only lie 15 per cent'. So, since then we have been lying only 15 per cent!

Marek's engine drove a four-speed, all-synchromesh gearbox through a 10in (254mm) diameter single, dry plate Borg and Beck clutch. The gearbox itself was built by David Brown and had baulk ring synchromesh on all forward gears, while the gear lever was a remote control unit which was centrally mounted at the back of the casing. The gears were closely grouped so that, with the standard final drive ratio 3.54:1, there were 3.31:1 and 2.93:1 options, the maximum speeds on the indirect ratios being 104mph, 85mph and 51mph (167kph, 136kph and 82kph).

LIVE REAR AXLE

The open propeller shaft drove the coil-sprung live Salisbury rear axle via a hypoid bevel final drive. This feature was effectively carried over from the DB2 and the twin tubular parallel arms therefore looked after the axle's fore and aft locations. There were, however, differences as the earlier Panhard rod was dispensed with and replaced by a Watts linkage, the swinging arm of which was attached to the banjo casing's cast-aluminium cover. This mechanism ensured that the axle had a true vertical movement. Unlike the DB2, where the coil springs were located in front of the axle, on the DB4 they were positioned behind it with their bases located in saddle pressings welded on either side of the casing. The advantage of this new layout was that each spring consequently was put in compression

The DB4's handsome badge proclaiming the company's ownership and hence its DB initials.

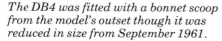

The DB4 was fitted with a bonnet scoop from the model's outset though it was reduced in size from September 1961.

These free-standing headlamps were used by the mainstream DB4 throughout its manufacturing life though those of its GT and Vantage contemporaries were cowled.

A 1963 Series 5 DB4 with higher roof line,
overall length extended to 15ft (4,572mm)
and 15 rather than 16in wheels.

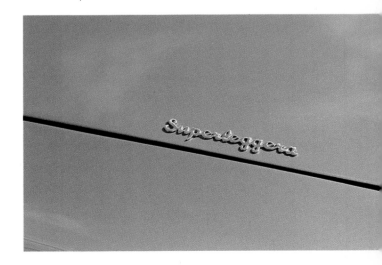

The badge, there was one either side of the
bonnet, which proclaimed that the
coachwork had been built in accordance
with Touring's Superleggera principles.

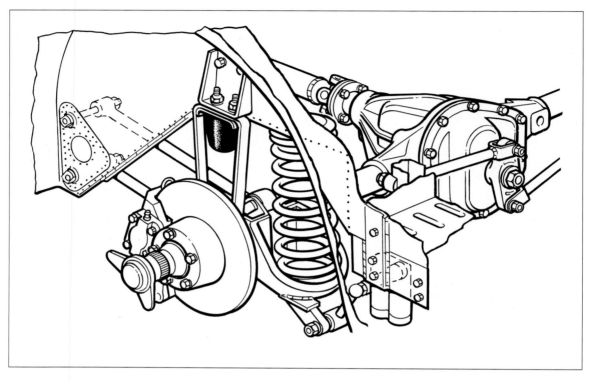

The trailing arm and coil spring rear suspension, which also incorporated a Watts linkage, as used on the DB4, DB5 and DB6.

when absorbing torque reaction, a useful refinement which came into its own when the car accelerated from a standstill. Armstrong lever-type shock absorbers were also employed.

For the independent front suspension, Harold Beach had opted for a more conventional coil-spring and wishbone layout. The top wishbones were shorter than the lower ones and were forgings which pivoted on maintenance-free rubber bushes. Between the two was a coil spring containing an Armstrong telescopic shock absorber. There was a further rear-mounted arm welded to the lower forging which completed the triangulation and which was attached to the chassis at its other end. A David Brown rack-and-pinion steering gear was mounted ahead of the suspension units which were joined by an anti-roll bar.

The DB Mark III had been fitted with Girling front disc brakes but the DB4 featured all-round discs of Dunlop manufacture. A Lockheed servo unit was fitted. The handbrake had separate mechanical callipers and was a fly-off unit located to the right of the driver. Wire wheels were carried over from the previous model, and the Dunlop centre locks were fitted with 6.00 × 16in Avon Turbospeed tyres as standard equipment.

FAST THINKING

The DB4 was shorter and lower than its DB2 predecessor; and with a larger carrying capacity, although surprisingly, in view of the amount of aluminium in the car, its dry weight of 25¾cwt (1,311kg) was about the

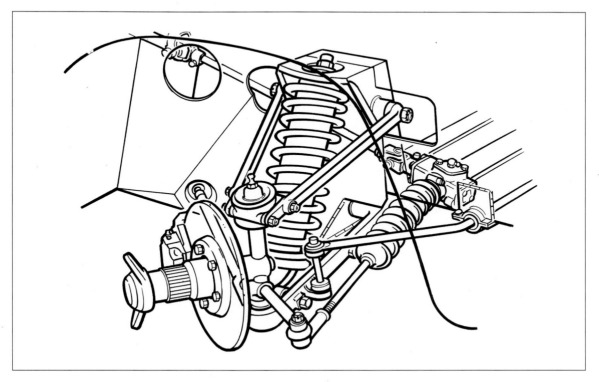

*Harold Beach's coil and wishbone independent front suspension,
introduced on the DB4 and also fitted to the DB5 and DB6.*

same as the DB2 which was probably on account of the platform chassis specified by Touring. It was also clearly faster than the DB2–4 although no independent road tests would be published until over two years after the car's announcement. Consequently, the motoring press could only estimate its top speed at the time of its arrival. *The Autocar* considered that 'its maximum speed is in excess of 140mph' while *The Motor* was rather more optimistic and said that the DB4 'offers road speeds of the order of 150mph'. The truth was that, in October 1958, Aston Martin only possessed two DB4s and these could only be considered to be pre-production prototypes. One car was needed for the model's motor show débuts and the firm could not entrust the remaining, and as yet unproven, example

to the motoring press. In these circumstances, John Wyer ingeniously came up with a headline-grabbing performance figure which would capture the public's attention.

Prior to the car's announcement Alan Dakers, Aston Martin's press and public relations manager, went to see Wyer to ask him whether there were any particular claims that could be made about the DB4's performance. The general manager thought for a moment and responded. 'You might say that it will accelerate from a standing start to 100mph and stop again in under 30 seconds.' A triumphant Dakers departed to incorporate this information in the DB4's advertising campaign, but the only trouble was that the calculation was a purely theoretical one! It was then a matter of

What other drivers got used to seeing: rear view of the 1963 DB4.

The quality of workmanship applied to the DB4's aluminium bodywork was, as this picture testifies, extremely high.

The rear of the 1963 DB4, the bumpers had lost their overriders by this time.

This rear light cluster was introduced for the 1962 model year.

Twin exhaust pipes had featured since the DB4's introduction. By this time the reflectors were bumper mounted.

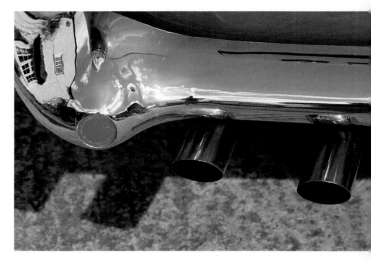

seeing whether the car could attain these figures.

So on 2 October, the day on which the Paris Motor Show opened, the second of the two DB4s the factory possessed at this time was at the Motor Industry Research Association's circuit at Lindley, Northamptonshire. Dr Albert Fogg, the track's director, had responded enthusiastically to Wyer's initiative and provided a research engineer to travel in the car to see fair play. Driven by Roy Parnell, the Aston Martin undertook a series of six tests and achieved the following results much, no doubt, to Wyer's relief: test 1, 27.4sec; test 2, 26.2sec; test 3, 27.8sec; test 4, 27.2sec; test 5, 27.4sec; test 6, 27.4sec; mean 27.2sec. These were carried out at one-minute intervals which reflected well on the Dunlop disc brakes, and the resulting MIRA certificate was duly incorporated in the DB4's advertisements.

LABOUR TROUBLES

Having received such an enthusiastic reception, Aston Martin could, at this stage, have sold every DB4 it could build. But before production could get under way, John Wyer became embroiled in a time-consuming inter-union dispute at Newport Pagnell which would prevent manufacture getting properly under way until the autumn of 1959. This is not the occasion to take a detailed look at the issue but it is, nevertheless, worth recording in outline because such industrial upheavals were an all too unhappy feature of the British motor industry in the 1960s, and affected such large companies as the BMC as well as specialist firms such as Aston Martin.

The problem basically related to the move to Newport Pagnell. By tradition, as a coach-building business, Tickford had been in the province of the National Union of Vehicle Builders (NUVB). Prior to Brown's purchase, the then management had agreed with the NUVB that it would be the only union with powers of negotiation at the factory. This agreement was in itself flawed because some members of the workforce belonged to the National Union of Sheet Metal Workers and Braziers, a state of affairs which the Vehicle Builders chose to ignore. But when David Brown bought the business in 1954 and decided to transfer car production there, it became necessary to recruit workers of differing skills, and these were members of the Amalgamated Engineering Union (AEU).

Once car production began at the former Tickford works, there was an uneasy truce between the NUVB and the larger AEU, and the latter was responsible for poaching some of its workers. This paved the way for a trial of strength between the two, the occasion for this being 1959 and the first year of DB4 production when demand was at its height for the new model. It was then that the NUVB chose to put the company under severe pressure.

The Union's contention was that, because the DB4 had a higher selling price than the DB2, its members should be paid more for building it. John Wyer, for the management, pointed out that in some respects it was easier and cheaper to manufacture than the previous model, and Aston Martin had never made a profit in the true sense of the word.

The DB4 chassis assembly line was the chosen site of the battle and, if the NUVB were to be victorious, this would clearly mean the end of the AEU at Newport Pagnell. The dispute lingered on throughout the summer of 1959 and, eventually, the NUVB conceded that if the management could demonstrate that the production times they had been set were attainable, they would accept them. In the end this is what happened.

MORE DEVELOPMENT

Although this dispute absorbed much of Wyer's time during the year, as it happened it did give the firm some breathing space so that it could undertake more development work on the DB4 to rectify some of its more obvious shortcomings. John Wyer had been the first to recognize that the car had, in fact, been introduced too soon because of pressure from Aston Martin dealers and David Brown, and said that although 'potentially a great sports car, it was completely lacking in detail refinement'. During 1959 the specification was therefore constantly uprated, and to have made these changes while the car was in production would have been prohibitively costly.

Production, as such, did not begin in earnest until after the NUVB dispute had been settled and almost a full year after the model's announcement. As had been the case with the DB Mark III, as much as possible was built at Newport Pagnell, although with the DB4 the exception was the platform chassis which hailed from the Huddersfield works of the David Brown Corporation. As the first cars began to come off the production line they were delivered to British customers, so that any problems could be within easy reach of rectification. Nevertheless the chief engineer, Harold Beach, was more than satisfied with the quality of work attained at the factory and, in particular, the standard of the bodywork produced there. He said:

Touring, apart from styling the car, also made the body tooling. The aluminium body panels were produced on a rubber press [by Dowty Bouton Paul]. Body engineering really was good as the Superleggera structure was extremely rigid and problems like doors dropping were absolutely unknown.

WORLD CHAMPIONS

If 1959 was significant for the year in which DB4 production started, it also represented a milestone in Aston Martin history as being the year in which the firm won the World Sports Car Championship, a triumph which can only have increased demand for the newly introduced road car.

During the winter of 1958/59, extensive work was undertaken on the DBR1 to ensure that it was to become sufficiently reliable to win Le Mans. All-important development was undertaken on the troublesome transaxle and, as a result of wind tunnel testing, the line of the tail was raised to improve air flow. But above all, the firm was determined to concentrate its resources on the 24-hour event and only enter that one race in the 1959 season.

The organizers of the Sebring 24-hour race in America then pleaded with Aston Martin to make an entry, stating that they could not run the race without them. Wyer reluctantly agreed to a shoe-string operation, although the DBR1 failed after thirty-two laps because of inadequate preparation.

Next, Stirling Moss asked to use a spare car for the Nurburgring 1,000-Kilometre Race. The factory agreed to transport the car and contributed team manager, Reg Parnell, and a couple of mechanics. Paying all his own expenses, Moss went on to win for the third year in succession.

LE MANS TRIUMPH

Then came Le Mans. At the 24-hour race the main challenge inevitably came from the V12 Ferraris, Jaguar having withdrawn from racing in 1956. Three DBR1s were entered, driven by Moss/Fairman, Salvadori/Shelby and Frère/Trintignant. Moss's car had a four-bearing crankshaft 255bhp engine while the other two were 240bhp seven-bearing units. In the race Moss kept the pressure up on the Ferraris, although in so doing he blew his engine up. The two leading Modena cars went out with blown cylinder head gaskets, but the third car still looked threatening. Salvadori and

Inlet side of the DB4's 3.7-litre Vantage engine which was fitted to most Series 5 DB4s

The DB4's door handles, courtesy of the Triumph TR series, were carried over for the DB5 and DB6.

The DB4 was the only model of the series to be fitted with manually operated windows. The DB5 and 6 had electric ones.

The DB4's Reutter seats were beautifully upholstered in Connolly leather and hinged to permit access to the rear.

The fine wood-rimmed steering wheel and comprehensive instrument panel were all part of the model's appeal. These Series 5 cars benefited from DB4 GT instrumentation with separate water temperature, oil pressure, fuel gauges and ammeter rather than the two dials that had previously sufficed.

Shelby led for much of the race but at 2 a.m. their car came into the pits suffering from rear-end vibration. Thoughts immediately turned to the trouble-prone transaxle but, thankfully, it transpired to be tyre trouble even though the delay cost Aston Martin the lead. The DBR1 would not regain it until around 10 a.m., and it was then that the third Ferrari blew a head gasket, and Salvadori and Shelby went on to win with a second DBR1 driven by Frère and Trintignant coming in second. Privately entered Ferraris occupied the next four places. After ten years, David Brown had achieved his objective of winning Le Mans.

Although Aston Martin had only intended to enter one race in 1959, the victory meant that the firm was now behind Ferrari and ahead of Porsche in the Sports Car Championship, and everything depended on the Tourist Trophy race at Goodwood which Aston Martin had won in the previous year. Three DBR1s were entered, but the Moss/ Salvadori car caught fire in the pits because, as Wyer had predicted, the refuelling apparatus was dangerous. The pit and the car were damaged, but manager Parnell brought in the Shelby/Farman car for Moss to drive, and Graham Whitehead sportingly withdrew his own DBR1 and let the firm have his pit. Moss went on to win and give Aston Martin the World Sports Car Championship which, at the beginning of the year, it had not even contemplated entering!

David Brown and John Wyer spontaneously decided that with this double triumph the time had come to withdraw from sports car racing so that the firm's resources could be concentrated on the production cars. The announcement was made at a victory dinner held at Helene Cordet's restaurant in London at the end of October.

FORMULA 1 FOLLY

Despite this decision, the firm decided to continue campaigning the DBR4, a front-engined Formula 1 car based on the DBR1 frame and 2½-litre version of the RB6 engine. The DBR4 had, in fact, been ready to race in 1958 but had not been used in view of the priority being given to the DBR1 programme. There were DB4 associations with the single seater because, in the winter of 1958/59, Ted Cutting redesigned its wishbone and torsion bar independent front suspension and replaced it with a DB4 layout. Despite a promising start at Silverstone in May 1959 when Salvadori finished second behind Brabham's rear-engined Cooper, the car thereafter proved to be a great disappointment and was rapidly overtaken, in every sense, by its lighter, rear-engined contemporaries. It evolved into DBR5 form in the following year, but the Formula 1 programme was wisely discontinued in the middle of 1960.

DB4 TROUBLES

It was at about this time that Aston Martin began to be plagued by a serious reliability problem on the DB4. During the winter of 1959/60, production was beginning to build up and cars were exported to Europe. In particular, they went to France via Marcel Blondeau, the firm's energetic distributor, and also to Italy. The trouble was bearing failure which usually meant a broken connecting rod and often seizure of the entire engine. As the number of complaints began to spiral, Wyer and his staff became apprehensive about answering the telephone or receiving a telegram. These reached a crescendo when four calls from France and a further three from Italy were received in quick succession.

John Wyer was particularly concerned about his discontented French customers because the market was a strong one and he had a good distributor in Blondeau. He immediately dispatched Tadek Marek to

Paris who was instructed, in no uncertain terms, not to return until he had found the solution. Two days after investigating the compaints, Marek rang Wyer who says that he told him: ' "I can only find one common factor between these failures." Full of excitement, I asked him what it was and he replied, "They all happened on Good Friday." ' Even though Wyer's sense of humour had been frayed by this time, he was still chuckling when he replaced the telephone receiver.

The root of the trouble lay in the use of the aluminium cylinder block, and fortunately it could be corrected. It was triggered by overheating and this occurred because it was a fault that had not been encountered during testing for, in view of a fundamental oversight, the DB4 had not been evaluated at sustained high speeds. Maximum speed tests had been undertaken at MIRA, but there had not been any testing on the banked high-speed circuit there. The fact that owners would want to use the cars for sustained, high-speed running was overlooked and was a reflection of the fact that, at the time of the DB4's gestation, Britain possessed no purpose-built motor road. The country's first motorway, the M1, did not open until November 1959, which was the first year of DB4 production and, in those days, there was no 70mph (113kph) speed limit – this did not arrive until 1967. British DB4 owners were soon following the example of their Continental contemporaries and opening up their cars down the new dual carriageway, some sharing the same fate as their European counterparts.

FLAT OUT IN FRANCE

Despite the fact that there were no autoroutes in France at this time, the string-straight *Routes Nationales* did lend themselves to sustained high-speed running, and young bloods delighted in setting

an unofficial record for the 120 miles (193km) between Paris and Le Mans.

Italy was another story. Not only was it hotter, but the purpose-built *autostradas* dated back to the 1920s and, just prior to the DB4's arrival, the *Autostrada del Sole* had just been opened between Milan and Bologna and was almost exactly the same distance as the Paris to Le Mans run. It was there that Italian enthusiasts in their Ferraris and Aston Martins were soon in the business of seeing who could drive fastest between the two cities. Traffic was light which meant that the cars could be driven flat out over the entire distance.

There was also an element of truth in Marek's quip about Good Friday. Easter was the first public holiday of the year in Europe and late March of 1959 was unusually warm, which gave car owners an opportunity to get out of the towns and into the country. There the combination of high temperatures and flat-out running played havoc with the DB4's engine.

The root of the problem lay in the fact that Aston Martin had had to use an aluminium crankcase rather than the more conventional cast-iron one. As a result, the clearances of the main bearings tended to expand as the engine got hotter. Marek later readily acknowledged this shortcoming:

It was possible to design a stiff engine with a stiff crankcase and a stiff crankshaft, but we didn't realize then that, when the engine gets hot, the clearances in the bearings can grow three times.

At 158°F (70°C) the oil requirement of the engine was much less than when it was running at 212°F (100°C) because, as the bearing clearances grew, much more oil was required. As the temperatures rose even higher and the bearings widened even more, a point was reached when the oil pump could no longer cope with demand because the clearance was too big. It circulated lubricant at the rate of about 20 gallons (88 litres) per minute and, when the engine was running flat out, this was the equivalent of the capacity of the sump being changed once every eight seconds. If it then became a matter of waiting for the oil to complete its circulation, the pump would suck air as well as oil with the same calamitous results.

GETTING IT RIGHT

Marek responded with a two-fold package. First, the engine was offered with an oil cooler as optional equipment on British cars and a total of eighty-eight cars were so equipped in 1960/61. This contributed to preventing the lubricant rising beyond the 212°F (100°C) mark. Second, adjustments were made to reduce the clearance so that there was not too much oil present when the engine got hot. Here it was a matter of balancing this with the amount required by the car if it was to start in cold weather when the oil was at its most viscous.

Once these modifications had been made, Aston Martin undertook an extensive programme of testing . . . on the M1. At this time the firm's tester was the former racing driver Bobby Dickson, who had been recommended to Wyer by Reg Parnell. Conveniently, Newport Pagnell was placed approximately half-way down the motorway and it was thought that such testing would be much closer to reproducing road conditions than at the MIRA circuit. An evaluation programme was soon under way. Dickson would leave the factory then turn north on to the M1 and remain on it until he reached Crick at its northern extremity. He then turned around and drove south down the entire length of the motorway to Watford. He then returned to the works, having covered 125 miles (201km).

Dickson completed the run regularly in under an hour, his record being 56 minutes, which represented an average speed of 133mph (214kph). One morning Wyer arrived

This stripped and lightened DB4, driven by Graham Warren and prepared by Goldsmith and Young, won the 1991 Chapman Warren Classic Car Championship.

at his office, spoke to Dickson, who was in the yard, made some telephone calls and, on looking out of the window, saw the test car at the pumps. So he went down and asked him why he had not yet started his run. Instead Dickson gave Wyer a hurt look and informed him: 'I've been . . .'

There were other, less sensational difficulties to resolve on these early DB4s in addition to the bearing problem. Complaints included

poor heating and ventilation, of the cars boiling in traffic and leaking in the rain, and some drivers disliked what they considered to be the heavy steering. All these peccadilloes took time to resolve and this, in their turn, delayed production.

This highlighted the fact that, as general manager, John Wyer was continually fighting a battle on two irreconcilable fronts. On one hand he was always under pressure from David Brown and his directors to increase production and, at the same time, he was being pressed to improve the DB4's quality and reliability, and to reduce the number of servicing complaints.

THE MODEL EVOLVES

Some of these modifications were incorporated into the Series 2 DB4s which arrived in January 1960. This, it should be noted, is not an official designation but one retrospectively devised by the Aston Martin Owners' Club to identify the various stages in the model's evolution. For the record, the Series 1 cars ran from chassis number DB4/101/R to DB4/250/L. Its successor began at DB4/251/L and lasted until April 1961 and chassis number DB4/600/R. The most noticeable change was that the bonnet was hinged at the front rather than at the rear to prevent

The Series 2 DB4 was introduced in January 1960 with a front- rather than rear-hinged bonnet, larger sump and improved front brakes. It remained in production in this form until April 1961.

it from being accidentally forced open by air pressure. Also, the sump capacity was increased from 15 to 17 pints (8.5 to 9.6 litres). The Series 2 DB4 proved to be the most numerically plentiful of the DB4 range, with 350 cars being built.

In view of these problems, very little appeared on the DB4 in the motoring press until early 1960. It was then that Laurence Pomeroy, as technical editor of *The Motor* and confidant of David Brown, published his first impressions of the car. He had been loaned the hard-working prototype 4 SMX during 1959 for his opinion, in particular, of its aluminium engine, an experience which was reported in his 'Account Rendered' of 3 February 1960. He found that in London he could hear the rear axle and found it kinder

to use second and third rather than third and top gears. Apart from this he made a ringing endorsement of the model by declaring: 'the DB4 is, in many ways, the safest and easiest car which I have ever driven'.

ROAD TESTING THE DB4

The Motor was also responsible for publishing the first full road test of the DB4 in its issue of 14 September 1960 (over a year ahead of its *Autocar* rival, which did not publish its test until October 1961). *The Motor* began its account by praising the steering:

Friction and flexibility are commonly regarded as being in some degree necessary features of a steering mechanism, to insulate the driver against road shocks, but the Aston Martin engineers have followed modern racing practice in eliminating both friction and lost motion almost completely. The rack and pinion mechanism is geared for quite quick response, needing only 2⅔ turns from lock to lock on a car with a 32½ feet [10m] turning circle.

Instant response to the driver's wishes is attained from this steering, at town speeds with quite large but easy wheel movements, or more sensitively upwards of two miles a minute. There is always plenty of castor action to provide feel, and the car has no tendency to wander off a straight course, but whilst the steering reacts to bumps it never kicks violently. At the last moment before delivery to us the test model was converted to the optional chrome-plated wheels [£73 13s 4d extra] and imperfect balancing of the new wheels and tyres caused marked shake of the steering wheel at speeds in the 50–60mph [80–96kph] region – although no discomfort was caused when 140mph [225kph] was exceeded. Reversion to more carefully balanced wheels after the first 850 miles [1,367km] of our test effected a great improvement.

Using Dunlop RS5 tyres, our test car cornered quite excellently on dry roads, showing a modest but comforting degree of understeer which was not greatly affected by throttle openings until enough power was applied for wheelspin to begin causing an outward drift to the tail. A very little body roll during very fast cornering probably serves a useful purpose to warning against attempts to take bends at utterly impossible speeds. It was a lot easier to slide the car or induce wheelspin when road surfaces were wet, but bad weather did not show up any vices in the race-bred chassis. The extra high tyre pressures recommended for competitive use or very fast motorway driving had little effect on riding comfort.

The magazine had this to say about riding comfort:

Paradoxically, it nowadays often seems true that 'grand touring' cars designed primarily for tenacious road holding also offer their passengers a steadier ride than do more ordinary saloons. Certainly this Aston Martin has a commendably versatile ability to negotiate either cobbled town streets or undulating main roads without discomfort to its passengers, especially when a full petrol tank or a little luggage softens the spring rates.

Exceptionally fast cars need exceptional brakes, and this car's Dunlop discs (with a vacuum servo in the hydraulic operating system) can lock the wheels at any speed with well under 100lb pressure on the pedal. The car's advertised ability to accelerate from rest to 100mph [160kph] and stop again in less than 30 seconds was demonstrable on less than half a mile of straight and level road, although the ease with which the wheels could be locked and a slight tendency for the test car's brakes to pull to the right invited snaking during such a severe trial. Even with the engine switched off and the gear lever in neutral to simulate a servo

failure there was still quite good brake power available in response to higher-than-usual pedal pressure. The not uncommon tendency for self-adjusting disc brakes to need extra travel for the first application after fast cornering is evident, but only to an innocuous extent. An excellent pull-up handbrake (with fly-off ratchet of racing pattern) is well placed outside the driving seat, and worked on the rear discs just well enough to hold the car on a 1 in 4 hill.

Luxury for two people has obviously been the primary objective of the body designer and, provided that there is room to open the wide doors, entry to the front seats is truly easy − getting up out of them can be less dignified. Rear-seat kneeroom depends on one or both seats being set reasonably well forward, but with no pedals ahead of it the passenger seat can almost always be set to leave comfortable room behind it for one man, and a second passenger can be carried if the driver is short legged or prepared to sacrifice his ideal seating position. Quite a good deal of luggage, in the form of ordinary rectangular cases, can be accommodated in a carpeted flat floored rear locker beneath which the spare wheel is hidden.

In most respects this car is furnished as a customer would expect, the fascia panel, for example being designed to cause no reflection in the windscreen but accommodating a lockable glove box and a full set of legible and substantially accurate instruments. The comfortable seats are well upholstered in leather, the floor is nicely carpeted, a map light supplements two interior lamps, the controls include finger-tip headlamp flasher buttons on each side of the steering wheel, and the electrical system is well protected by eight fuses. Utterly unexpected simplifications are the absence of door operated courtesy switches for the interior lights, and of any self cancelling for the flashers. Calibration of the fuel gauge merely in quarters of a tankful is a pity, but one must praise the range given by the 19 gallon [105 litre] tankage, the peace of mind given by a petrol reverse tap on the fascia, and a filler which lets any fuel pump be run at full speed.

On light and air, *The Motor* said:

Long-range headlamps permit fast travel over empty roads late at night, but their truly non dazzle dipped beam demanded a much lower speed when meeting other traffic. An interior heating system provides plenty of warmed fresh air for anyone who can master the six controls provided – a task which the instruction manual does little to simplify! Our test car had the optional Motorola twin speaker push button radio, which if not always mellow could produce enough volume of sound to be very audible at any speed in any gear.

Having said all this, one must come back to the remarkable performance which a top speed of about 2½ miles [4km] a minute

This Goldsmith and Young-prepared DB4 and a similar sister car are, at the time of writing (1991), the only racing Aston Martins running with engines bored out to 4.5 litres.

The alloy roll cage is an all-important fitment in this racing DB4 in which the model's handsome lines remain unsullied.

highlights. 139.3mph [224kph] was recorded on the 3.54 axle ratio normally used for Europe, an even livelier 3.77 ratio being used for the U.S.A. where most motorways have a speed limit. At top speed, the engine was exceeding 6,000rpm and hesitancy was perceptible (power falls off beyond 5,500rpm) and obviously the 3.31 axle which is available for those few customers who value top speed above all else would have permitted an even higher timed speed. Sustaining more than 6,000rpm for a series of timed runs over the measured mile, slight, temporary loss of oil pressure was noted despite an optional oil cooler being on our

test car, but 120mph [193kph] at 5,300rpm seemed to be a happy cruising speed.

The broad range of speed over which this engine gives very strong torque is indicated by closely similar top gear acceleration times recorded at very dissimilar speeds; from 10 to 30mph [16–48kph] in 8.2sec, from 50 to 70mph [80–113kph] in 8.4sec or from 90 to 110mph [149–177kph] in 9.2sec. The unheated induction system which asks for a little warming up after the engine has been started each morning (a radiator blind is provided to accelerate this process) does not really give smooth running at *steady* speeds below 30mph [48kph] in top gear, although acceleration from much lower speeds is possible in this ratio.

Despite its substantial engine size, this car does not show its true form until the indirect gears are used to some extent. At the suggested limit of 5,800rpm which is by no means fussy, the lower ratios provide speeds of 52, 75 and 105mph, [84, 121 and 169kph] so that there is a suitable ratio for leaping promptly and safely past other traffic at any speed. Although, when revving, the engine will swing the car up a gradient of 1 in 3½ in second gear, an otherwise very firm clutch slips if too many engine r.p.m. are used for a start from rest and limits first gear re-start abilities to a 1 in 4 slope as well as preventing 240 net bhp producing quite as dynamic a rest-to-30mph [48kph] time as might expected. Once the wheels are turning, however, the speed rises in magnificent style, 60mph [96kph] being reached in 9.3sec and 120mph [193kph] in 31½sec.

Without pretending to be a silent touring model, this very fast saloon is quiet enough internally for conversation to continue at very high road speeds, and a healthy exhaust note never becomes objectionable. The close ratio gears are all fairly quiet, and third is so silent that on a winding road the driver can easily forget that he is not in top gear. Synchromesh on all ratios is effective, but the clutch pedal has to be depressed all the way if drag was not to occur. Fuel consumption figures in the middle teens of m.p.g. can be expected, and whilst the engine prefers 100-octane fuel, it will tolerate any premium petrol.

Performance, controllability and comfort have combined in the Aston Martin DB4 to make it a highly desirable car; one in which long journeys can be completed very quickly indeed with the minimum of risk or discomfort, and the maximum of pleasure.

The Motor provided the following figures for maximum speeds:

Flying Mile
Mean of four opposing runs
139.3mph [223.6kph]
Best one-way time equals
140.9mph [226.7kph]

'Maximile' speed (Timed ¼ mile [0.4km] after 1 mile [1.6km] accelerating from rest)
Mean of four opposing runs
130.2mph [209.5kph]
Best of one-way time equals
132.4mph [213.07kph]

Acceleration times from standstill

0–30mph [51kph]	4.3sec
0–40mph [64kph]	5.7sec
0–50mph [80kph]	7.2sec
0–60mph [96kph]	9.3sec
0–70mph [113kph]	11.4sec
0–80mph [129kph]	13.6sec
0–90mph [145kph]	16.7sec
0–100mph [161kph]	20.1sec
0–110mph [177kph]	24.5sec
0–120mph [193kph]	31.5sec
Standing ¼ mile [0.4km]	16.8sec

MORE CHANGES

In April 1961, six months after this test was published, Aston Martin introduced further modifications and improvements to the DB4. These Series 3 changes only applied in 1961 and ran from chassis numbers DB4/601/R to DB4/765/R in September of that year. The most significant fitting was the arrival of overdrive as an option on the model, a device which, it will be recalled had featured on the DB Mark III and not carried over for the DB4. The three alternative rear axle ratios were perpetuated through the Laycock de Normanville unit, and was only available with the 3.77:1 and 4.09:1 ones. This, claimed the factory, meant a cruising speed of 120mph (193kph) at 4,700rpm, with the car's maximum speed increased to 147mph

(236kph) in overdrive top with the lowest of the ratios.

Cars, like people, tend to put on weight as they get older and to reduce this and improve rigidity, lighter bodywork was introduced. Up until then, the DB4s were made of half-hard aluminium and this was replaced by two sets of lighter panels, in 1.26 and 2 per cent aluminium magnesium. At the same time came triple rear light clusters and twin bonnet stays. Improved sound-deadening material was introduced into the car and there was a new silencer to reduce internal noise levels.

In view of customer complaints, the output of the heater was increased and the demister facilities improved with five outlets in place of the original three. An electric tachometer took the place of the mechanical unit previously employed. Changes were also made to the controls: there was a new switch and control arm which combined the functions of the headlamp flasher, dipping and turn indicator signals. The windscreen wiper blades were also redesigned to improve their efficiency at speeds up to 120mph (193kph). The engine was unchanged, although at number 370/571 came an all-important modification with the arrival of a 21pt (12-litre) sump.

A CONVERTIBLE VERSION

Unlike the Mark III, which was available as a coupé and drophead coupé, for the first three years of its life the DB4 was only available in closed form. This deficiency was remedied at the 1961 Paris and London Motor Shows when Aston Martin unveiled its open version, although the drophead coupé name, rooted as it was in the pre-War years, was dispensed with so this new model was known as the DB4 Convertible. Touring did not want the job, so it was engineered by Harold Beach, and the former technical director of Mulliner Park Ward, George Moseley. At £4,449, it was £364 more than the coupé which by then sold for £4,085. The PVC hood, which one person could raise and lower, contained a large plastic rear window which was somewhat larger than that fitted to the coupé. There was also a fully trimmed steel hard-top available which could be used in winter.

The introduction of a folding hood meant that the petrol tank, located behind the rear seat, was dispensed with and replaced by twin tanks positioned respectively in each rear wing. These had a combined capacity of 16 gallons (73 litres) which was 3 gallons (13 litres) less than that of the coupé. Inevitably this reduced luggage space, although the boot was extended to give approximately the same capacity. Rear seat width was the same as the closed car but shoulder space was reduced somewhat.

In view of the lack of a roof, the under-structure of the chassis was strengthened by the introduction of heavy-duty sills, and the bulkheads behind the engine and the rear seat was also reinforced. This added about 50lb (23kg) to the weight of the open car, bringing it up to around 27cwt (1,374kg). The exterior of the convertible otherwise closely resembled that of the coupé, although there was a new grille, with seven vertical bars and the bonnet scoop was reduced in size. These features were also extended to the closed car for the 1962 season.

RETURN OF THE VANTAGE

At the same time that the convertible made its début, Aston Martin introduced what it described as the triple carburettored Special Series engine. This effectively represented a half-way house between the standard unit and that of the potent, short chassis GT version which had arrived in 1959, and

A left-hand drive DB4 Vantage, with distinctive cowled headlamps, pictured at the 1962 Paris Show for the 1963 season.

which is described in Chapter 4. As Tadek Marek reflected:

We decided that we couldn't do any more with two SU carburettors, so we put a three carburettor system on the engine and this developed just under 240bhp. This was the so called 'Special Series' engine and that was as far as the 3.7 litre engine was developed in production form ... We felt we had to have a unit that was driveable, say, from 1,000rpm upwards in top gear ... and not a unit that would only start to pull about 3,500rpm in town.

In addition to the aforementioned triple SUs, the cylinder head employed the GT's larger valves, the compression ratio was upped from 8.2:1 to 9:1 and an oil cooler was a standard fitting. The engine was optimistically said to have developed 266bhp (net) at 5,750rpm, although as Marek had pointed out, the true figure was less than 240bhp but output was greater than that of the standard car and the GT below 4,000rpm. The Vantage name, which had first appeared on the DB2, was revived for this model which was instantly identifiable as the headlamps were recessed and protected with perspex covers to improve aerodynamic

The same Vantage DB4 at the 1962 Paris Show in profile with the headlamp treatment of the standard DB4 in the foreground.

efficiency, a feature which had first appeared on the GT car.

Other minor modifications included a redesigned throttle linkage, and the instrument panel was similar to that of the GT and was fitted with an oil temperature gauge which was not specified on the standard coupé, although it did appear on the 1963 model year cars. The Vantage cost £4,230 which was only £145 more than the basic version.

SERIES IMPROVEMENTS

The Series 5 car of September 1962 represented the ultimate version of the DB4.

These began at chassis number DB4/1001/L for the standard cars. The Vantage cars ran from DB4/1111/L to DB4/1165/R and from DB4/1176 to 1215/L. The Convertibles started at DB4C/1081/L and ran to DB4C/1110/L and from DB4C/1166/R to 1175/L. Although the wheelbases remained the same, the body itself was about 3½in (89mm) longer at around 15ft (4,572mm) and was slightly higher with more room for the rear passengers. This improved both foot and luggage accommodation. A thermostatically controlled fan was introduced to reduce the engine noise and 15in (381mm) wheels replaced the original 16in (406mm) ones, these being fitted with 6.70 × 15 tyres. The first fifty examples of the Series 5 model

The Series 5 DB4 was in production between September 1962 and June 1963 and this is the popular Vantage variant which paved the way to the DB5.

were fitted with the standard engine, although from then on and until the model ceased production in 1963, almost all cars were fitted with the SS unit and its distinctive, faired-in headlamps.

By the time that DB4 production ceased in June 1963 (at DB4/1050/R for the coupé and DB4/1165/R on the Vantage while the last open car of the series was DB4C/1175/L), a total of 1,100 cars had been built of which seventy were convertibles. This made the DB4 the most numerically successful Aston Martin ever built and exceeded total DB2 production which ran for a nine-year period. After a difficult start, the DB4 was becoming increasingly reliable as faults were ironed out. But as will be apparent, it was also available in more potent sports racing forms – and these desirable versions will be considered in the next chapter.

4 Faster: GT, Zagato and Other Projects

'In sheer performance there are not more than a half dozen road cars in the world which can match the agility of this special-bodied Aston Martin.'
The Autocar (on the DB4 GT Zagato), 13 April 1962.

Despite the fact that the DB4 was first and foremost a road car, there were a number of exciting sports racing derivatives: the visually similar short chassis GT; an exotic Zagato-bodied version; and three so-called 'Project' cars which were all related, in varying degrees, to the DB4 design.

The GT, which was designated Design Project 199, appeared in prototype form on 2 May 1959 in the first GT race to be held at Silverstone. Run in the morning before the crowds began to build up, Stirling Moss had little opposition and won easily from Roy Salvadori in a Coombs 3.4-litre Jaguar. This was the same International Trophy meeting at which the DBR4 single seater provided such an impressive first showing, although it was to prove to be a false dawn.

Next came Le Mans and this was the year of Aston Martin's celebrated victory. In addition to the trio of DBR1s, the firm also entered the same DB4 GT to be run as a prototype. As the 3-litre limit was in force, the 3.7-litre engine was replaced by the short stroke 92 × 72mm, 2,992cc unit which had previously been used in the sports racing DBR3. This required fairly extensive modifications to the car because the engine was a dry-sump unit and its tank had to be placed in the boot. Moss was later to reflect that the GT was fitted with so many pipes and pumps that it resembled a mobile oil refinery!

It was driven by Patthey, Aston Martin's Swiss distributor, and he was to share the wheel with Calderari and with Renaud as reserve. During practice it was found that the GT's petrol consumption was greater than had been anticipated, so the tank's capacity was increased from 32 to 38 gallons (145 to 211 litres). In the event, Patthey only lasted for twenty laps and withdrew on the twenty-first with suspected bearing failure.

This was subsequently put down to inadequate development and a lack of testing of the re-engined car. The withdrawal was also a recognition by Aston Martin that the 3-litre version of the DB4 was not a sound concept. In retrospect, the firm considered it to be too long and heavy, the block too high, the connecting rod/stroke ratio too great, and the connecting rods and pistons overweight which was to result, for two events running, in bearing failure.

The DB4 GT was announced in October 1959, a year after the arrival of DB4 proper and, at £4,534, it was a substantial £779 more. Despite the fact that it resembled the mainstream model, the GT was in fact 5in (127mm) shorter with a wheelbase of 7ft 9in (2,362mm). This meant dispensing with the rear seat which was replaced with a simple luggage shelf. The body also weighed less, the panels were made of 18 gauge magnesium aluminium and the car turned the scales at 24.1cwt (1,230kg) which was 178lb (80kg) less than the standard car. Lightweight centre-lock Borrani wire wheels,

Close-up of the radiator. This grille is unlike any other fitted new to a Zagato.

This side view of the car's front, revealing its unique 'shark's mouth' radiator.

Bonnet bulges were necessary to clear the engine's cam boxes.

This 1962 DB4 GT Zagato,
0190L, was the left-hand drive
car in which Roy Salvadori won
his class and was placed second
overall in the BRSCC Brands
Hatch meeting in 1962.

The all-important engine
compartment air outlet
enhanced by the Zagato badge.

Aston Martin's official picture of the short wheelbase DB4 GT, as it appeared in 1959. It was distinguished by its deeper bonnet scoop, cowled headlamps and lightweight Borrani wheels.

with distinctive three- rather than two-eared knock-off caps were fitted.

POTENT GT

The GT's engine was said to develop 302bhp at 6,000rpm, although the true figure was 267bhp. It differed from the DB4 in a number of important respects. The twin overhead camshaft six was lighter, the head and crankcase/block assembly being made of RR50 alloy. Ignition was by twin sparking plugs per cylinder, ignited via two distributors driven at right angles from the rear of the camshafts. The original twin SU carburettors were dispensed with and replaced by three Weber DCO E4 twin choke units. The camshafts were special high-lift ones and the engine had a 9:1 compression ratio. To cope with this increased power, a 9in (229mm) twin rather than single 10in (254mm) plate clutch was fitted. The gearbox was a close ratio unit and a Salisbury Powr-Lok limited slip differential was standardized. Five rear axle ratios were specified.

The brakes differed from those fitted to the DB4 in that while those were all-round

The GT's engine, prepared for display purposes with triple Weber 45 DCOE4 carburettors. The 3.7-litre engine developed 272bhp at 6,000rpm, despite what the notice proclaimed!

The back of the GT's engine showing the camshaft-driven distributors servicing the twin-plug cylinder head.

Dunlop discs, on the GT there were larger diameter Girling units of the variety used in the competition cars. A servo unit was not fitted.

The GT was intended to be a sports racer but it was also a desirable, if noisy, road car, so the quality of the interior was up to the usual Aston Martin standards. The boot was mostly occupied by the spare wheel and a 30-gallon (136-litre) light alloy petrol tank, although a few were fitted with twin wing-mounted units.

In a headline-grabbing test which echoed the one that had heralded the arrival of the DB4, a similar feat was undertaken with the GT, although the faster model was able to accelerate from rest to 100mph (161kph) and stop again in 20 rather than 30 seconds. Once again held at MIRA, and with a driver and observer on board, two successful runs were made, both of which were timed at 20 seconds which suggests that this test proved to be rather more difficult to undertake than the earlier one. In these instances, the 100mph (161kph) mark was reached in 14.8 and 14.6 seconds.

GT production began at chassis number DB4GT/0101/L and lasted until March 1963 and DB4/GT/0201/L, apart from numbers 0192 and 0194 to 0198. Of these, a total of seventy-five GTs were produced, of which six were special lightweight cars.

THE ESSEX CONNECTION

Aston Martin had retired from sports racing

The purposeful front end of the Zagato with supplementary air intake for the oil cooler below the radiator.

The Zagato's door handles clearly differed from those of its DB4 GT Touring bodied contemporary.

Although the Zagato was an out and out sports racer, the cars were nicely trimmed.

Detail of one of the two petrol filler caps which were located in either wing.

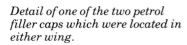

The DB4 GT pictured at the 1960 London Motor Show. By this time the headlamps cowls had acquired surrounds. Rear view (below) of the 1960 show car displaying its twin petrol fillers supplying the 30-gallon (136-litre) tank, which occupied most of the boot space. Only front seats were fitted.

A left-hand drive DB4 GT, pictured at the 1961 Geneva Motor Show.

by the time that the DB4 GT appeared, although works support was given to John Ogier's newly established Essex Racing Stable. Initially it campaigned two lightweight GTs, 0125 and 0151, subsequently registered 18 TVX and 17 TVX. These were entered in the 1960 Tourist Trophy race held at Goodwood in August, and were driven by Roy Salvadori and Innes Ireland. There was also a corporate presence in the form of team manager, Reg Parnell, along with Aston Martin mechanics. Salvadori drove an excellent race and, on occasions, was ahead of Moss in Rob Walker's Ferrari. Then his nearside rear wheel collapsed and he crawled back to the pits on the brake disc, although he did go on to achieve a well-earned second place behind Moss. Innes Ireland was third in the other GT.

Moss himself had run a GT on three other occasions in addition to his drive in the prototype. Across the Atlantic at Nassau in the West Indies, in November 1959, he had

driven an example owned by Frank de Arellano of San Juan, Puerto Rico. There he won the five-lap GT heat ahead of Roy Salvadori, but the car failed in the final when he was in the lead. Then in 1960 at Easter Goodwood, and at the wheel of Equipe Endeavour's noisy GT, he once again beat Salvadori, who was this time driving a 3.8-litre Jaguar.

In October came the Montlhery 1,000-kilometre race and the Essex Racing Team entered two GTs, one driven by Salvadori and Innes Ireland, and the other by Jim Clark and Tony Maggs. There was a formidable challenge from a host of Ferrari GTOs, and although Salvadori was fastest in practice, it was the cars from Modena that set the pace. Then Roy's GT began to understeer badly as he went into a fast S-bend, once

(Overleaf) *The Zagato's glorious and timeless lines revealed in side view. This car is owned by Aston Martin spares specialists, Aston Service Dorset Ltd, of Wimborne, Dorset.*

Stirling Moss at the wheel of lightweight DB4 GT 0124/R, winning at 83.03mph (133.62kph), the Fordwater Trophy race for closed cars at Goodwood on Easter Monday, 1961.

again a wheel had collapsed although this time it was a front one. Salvadori was ready to abandon the car but he was urged to get the GT into the pits by the omnipresent Marcel Blondeau, Aston Martin's French distributor, so he limped to sanctuary on his car's brake disc. There a new wheel was fitted and Salvadori went on to complete the race and came in sixth behind no less than five Ferraris. Clark and Maggs had retired, despite having at one stage reached fourth position, after a valve remained open during a pit stop and holed a piston when the engine was restarted.

FASTER ZAGATO

DB4 GTs continued to be campaigned in mainly second-string events because, from thereon, they were overshadowed by a more potent and lighter Zagato-bodied version which appeared at that company's first ever stand at the 1960 London Motor Show.

Like Touring the Zagato company, established in 1919, was also based in Milan. Initially Ugo Zagato, its founder, had been responsible for the distinctive lines which were conceived in conjunction with his sheet metal workers. This was the traditional method of producing bodies and it continued in the post-war years. However, Zagato had to move with the times and, after the war, Ugo's two sons, Elio and Gianni, were responsible for modernizing the firm, and introduced a sense of order and advanced planning to the company's activities. The first design of this new era was by 23-year-old Ercole Spada, who was to be responsible for styling all Zagato's bodies until 1969. His first essay was the Alfa Romeo Guilia-based TZ1 coupé. The next to appear was on another Alfa Romeo floorpan in the shape of the sports racing SZ version of the Guilietta, which was unveiled at the 1960 Geneva Show and, in some respects, can be seen as the precursor of the Aston Martin design.

Carrozzeria Zagato

The firm that was responsible for bodying this most famous version of the DB4 GT was, like Touring, Milan based although thankfully it survives to this day.

Like so many Italian coach-building establishments, the firm is essentially the story of one man. Ugo Zagato was born in 1890 and, as an eighteen-year-old in 1908, he went to Milan to join the Varesina coach-building firm. He became its superintendent, although at the age of twenty-five he left and then joined the Pomilio aircraft company in Turin. It was during his spell there, in the First World War, that Zagato learned the importance of light, strong construction which he applied when he established his own coach-building business in 1919. Initially Fiat and Ansaldo cars were so bodied, although he soon established an association with Alfa Romeo. Much of Zagato's subsequent reputation was built on the superlative open two-seater (spyder) body it built on the 1750 6C chassis from 1928, even though the lines were the work of the factory's Luigi Fusi.

With the end of the Second World War Ugo's eldest son, Elio, joined the firm and, in 1955, he was followed by his younger brother Gianni. They were to take over the running of the business and introduced long-overdue modernization. Zagato continued its relationship with Alfa Romeo and contributed the chunky 1900 SSZ of 1955, with similarly executed versions of the Giulietta Sprint.

It was in 1960 that twenty-three-year-old Ercole Spada was taken on, and he was responsible for the lines of the Aston Martin DB4 Zagato. He also designed the Zagato bodywork for the Lancia Flavia, Flaminia and Fulvia and the SZ, TZ and Junior Z for Alfa Romeo and OSCA 1600 GT. When he left in 1970 his place was taken by Giuseppe Mittino. The concept of the Aston Martin Zagato was revived in 1985 on the V8 chassis and was limited to 50 cars. In 1991 the firm was also responsible for re-creating the legendary DB4 Zagato in Sanction II form (*see* boxed feature on page 104).

Unlike the Touring-bodied cars which were built under licence at Newport Pagnell, the Zagato DB4 GTs were bodied by that company in Italy at its premises at 16 Via Giorgini, Milan. On completion, the majority of them were returned to the Aston Martin factory for trimming, although Zagato did complete a few left-hand drive examples itself. The model's 9.7:1 compression ratio engine was a more powerful version than that used in the Touring-styled GT and was said by the factory to develop 314bhp, although the true figure was actually 285bhp.

MOTOR SHOW DÉBUT

The wickedly purposeful silver-grey prototype which appeared at Earls Court was actually the final number of the series, chassis number 0220R. This was a well-known ploy (of which Ferrari was the chief

practitioner) to convince the authorities that the necessary 100 cars had been completed over a twelve-month period to conform with Appendix J Group 2 rulings. In fact a mere nineteen Zagatos were built. They were split almost evenly between right- and left-hand drive cars which accounted for ten and nine respective examples. One chassis (0201L) was fitted with a Bertone coupé body in 1961. The chassis numbers fell within the DB4 GT allocation and ran from 0176R to 0200R, although four of them were not used (0192 and 0196 to 0198) until nearly thirty years later, in 1991.

Once again it was John Ogier's stable that campaigned the Zagatos with greatest verve. He ordered two examples which were delivered in mid-1961 just prior to Le Mans, and which were memorably registered 1 VEV (0182R) and 2 VEV (0183R). They were to be driven, respectively, by Jack Fairman and Bernard Consten and a visiting

Like the Touring-bodied cars, the Zagato's boot contained a 30-gallon (136-litre) petrol tank and spare wheel.

At some stage in its career, this Zagato has been fitted with twin Scintilla magnetos in place of the original distributors.

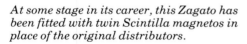

The rear light cluster varied from car to car.

The Sanction II Zagato's engine, which differed from the original's in being 4.2 rather than 3.7 litres.

The wood-rimmed steering wheel and instruments are essentially similar to the Touring-bodied GTs.

The original matt black finish. There is plenty of safety padding around the windscreen.

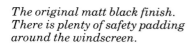

This left-hand drive DB4 GT, 0201L in Zagato series but with Bertone coachwork, pictured at the 1961 Geneva Show. Christened Jet by Bertone, it also appeared in the Turin Show later in the same year.

A left-hand drive DB4 Zagato, displayed at the 1961 Geneva Motor Show. Note the coachbuilder's Z monogram, just ahead of the air intake on the front wing.

Australian duo from the Kangaroo Stable, Lex Davison and Bob Stilwell. There was a third Zagato DB4 at Sarthe, the French-entered left-hand drive 0180L in which Jean Kerguen and Claude 'Franc' Dewez shared the driving.

Unfortunately, the Ogier-entered Zagatos dropped out, both infuriatingly having blown their head gaskets after a mere two and a half hours of running. The cylinder head nuts on the engines of both cars had not been torqued down between practice and the race itself, but then they had been run in on the test bed and, in theory, were all set to go. The left-hand drive car faired better but withdrew with a jammed starter when in ninth position – its cylinder head nuts had been tightened prior to the race. Ogier also entered a DBR1, driven by Roy Salvadori and Tony Maggs, and there was a second example for Border Reivers which was shared by Jim Clark and Ron Flockhart. This withdrew early on with engine trouble, although the Essex car lasted until the eighteenth hour and was in fourth place when a damaged fuel tank forced its retirement.

TEAM AWARD

At a GT race at Aintree prior to the British Grand Prix in July, Davison won in 2 VEV and beat Jack Sears' E-type, that famous Jaguar model having been introduced earlier in the year, while Sir John Whitmore was second in a GT from the same stable. The Tourist Trophy race at Goodwood in August proved to be an important occasion for the Zagato. Roy Salvadori drove 1 VEV and Jim Clark drove 2 VEV, while Innes Ireland took the wheel of a standard bodied GT. The race was dominated by Ferraris driven into first and second place respectively by Stirling Moss and Mike Parkes, but the works-supported Ogier team all completed the race with Salvadori coming in third, Clark fourth and Ireland fifth, Essex

Racing Services winning the team prize. This was a good showing, particularly as the ERS pitwork was slower than the Ferrari one and the Zagato consumed tyres at a much faster rate – Salvadori alone got through fourteen covers during the three-hour race.

In September Ogier entered 1 VEV in the GT event held at Monza prior to the Italian Grand Prix. Driven by Tony Maggs, he came in a creditable second place behind the inevitable Ferrari 250, and Kerguen was placed fourth in his Zagato.

At the 1,000-kilometre event at Montlhery in October, Ogier once again fielded 1 VEV and 2 VEV, driven by Clark and Ireland, and Maggs and Sir John Whitmore. Both cars suffered from fuel vaporization which interrupted their progress, although they did finish in sixth and ninth places.

Zagatos continued to be campaigned into 1962 as other examples were purchased by private owners. E.H.B. Portman ran 0177R in BARC and Aston Martin's Owners' Club events, and 0190L was bought new by John Coombs with Roy Salvadori driving it at a BRSCC meeting at Brands Hatch in May. Alas, it proved no Ferrari beater, and Salvadori believed that it would require a great deal of 'sorting' to become competitive as he finished in what he considered to be a poor second place to Innes Ireland's Ferrari GTO in the Peco Trophy race. Coombs did not run the Zagato again. However, by this time Aston Martin was preparing a purpose-built single car to run at Le Mans in 1962, not with any real hope of winning but, as John Wyer has put it, for reconnaissance.

PROJECT 212

Despite the fact that Aston Martin had been officially out of sports car racing since 1959, Wyer soon found himself under pressure from Marcel Blondeau in France to return to Le Mans in order to give Aston Martin sales

DB4 Zagato 0180R, memorably registered 1 VEV by Essex Racing Stables, uncharacteristically stationary at a British race meeting.

a boost there. So, in the first week of February 1962, he summoned Ted Cutting to his office and asked him to have a car ready for Le Mans. This was a little over four months away, and he wanted it three weeks prior to the event which was scheduled for the weekend of 15 and 16 June. The resulting car carried the DP 212 designation and, as it never reached production status, it has always been so known. Project 212 was, in fact, ready two weeks before the race, which represented a considerable achievement on Cutting's part.

His brief from Wyer was to use the DB4 GT as its basis, but with a five-speed gearbox

and a de Dion rear axle with outboard disc brakes. The car had a wheelbase of 7ft 10in (2,388mm) and it was 1in (25.4mm) longer than the standard GT. The 4ft 6in (1,372mm) front and rear track was, however, the same. As there was a new class for 4-litre prototypes in the race, the engine's bore was upped from 92 to 96mm, which gave a capacity of 3,996cc, a size which had first appeared in the Lagonda Rapide of the previous year. The block was cast in LM 230 aluminium alloy, the valves enlarged and three two-choke Weber 50 DCO carburettors were used. Inlet manifolds were of light alloy while the exhaust

The Zagato's distinctive bumperless rear showing the twin petrol filler caps.

system was made from large-diameter Inconel pipe. With its customary optimism, Aston Martin claimed that this engine developed 345bhp at 6,000rpm, although in reality the true figure was 327bhp. Because of the use of the GT chassis, the twin cam six was mounted in the customary DB4 position which Cutting considered to be too far forward. The five-speed gearbox, with a magnesium alloy casing, was mounted in unit with it.

DE DION REAR

The front suspension of the car was essentially the DB4 layout, although the upper wishbones were extended and the pivot points altered to give more camber change. At the rear was a de Dion rear axle, courtesy of the DB4-based Lagonda Rapide. It had a final drive ratio of 3.27:1. This was used in conjunction with the torsion bar and trailing links of the DBR2 – fortunately a spare set had been made. A Watts linkage took care of lateral location. Disc brakes by Girling were fitted all round and were 12in (305mm) at the front and 11.4in (289mm) at the rear. Lightweight Borrani wire wheels were used with 600–16 tyres at the front and 6.50–16 ones at the back.

When the drilled chassis, with its distinctive

aluminium floorpans, was completed it was dispatched complete with dummy engine to Newport Pagnell to be bodied. Cutting had produced a sketch of the sort of coupé he wanted and the draughtsman, Steve Stephens, went up to Buckinghamshire to supervise the work which was undertaken in a mere two or so weeks by a talented sheet-metal worker named Bert Brooks. It was built up from 22 gauge alloy sheet mounted on 20 gauge steel tubes. As speed was of the essence, only about a third of the jigs used on the DBR1 programme were used.

The finished product was a unique two-door coupé and bore some resemblance to the Zagato, although outwardly it was a four-seater with a distinctive tail and was 6in (152mm) longer than the Italian body at 14ft 6in (4,420mm). It was also appreciably lighter than the Zagato and weighed 19.2cwt (975kg) compared with 23cwt (1,170kg).

As Project 212 was not ready in time for the Le Mans test weekend of 7 and 8 April, Essex Racing Service's 2 VEV was fitted with its 4-litre engine, even though it was only running with a 8.2:1 compression ratio as its special pistons were not yet ready. Nevertheless it managed the second fastest time of the day and lapped at 4 min 12.9 sec which was equivalent to an average of 121.2mph (195.04kph), and its best speed over the timed stretch was 162mph (261kph). This was only bettered by Willy Mairesse in Noblet's Ferrari 250 GT who was 4mph (6kph) and 5.8 sec faster. There was another Zagato presence in the shape of Kerguen's Swiss entered car but, with its 3.7-litre engine, it was both quieter and slower than 2 VEV, its fastest lap being 114.4mph (184.1kph).

A BODY BLOW

Project 212 was ready in time for the race

and it was driven by Graham Hill and his BRM team-mate, Richie Ginther. Practice was outwardly uneventful, although Hill was disturbed to find that the rear of the car was leaving the ground down the Mulsanne straight when he was achieving over 180mph (290kph).

In the race proper Hill made a good start and succeeded in leading the race for a lap. The 212 remained in second place but, at the end of the first hour, it fell back to have its dynamo armature changed. The car soon returned to the fray but retired after five hours of running with a dropped valve which had resulted in a hole in number six piston. More seriously, the handling problem that Hill had experienced showed that something was amiss with the car's aerodynamics.

This Project car was not the only Aston Martin running at Sarthe in 1962. Zagato 0193R was driven by Jean Kerguen and 'Franc', but it dropped out after 134 laps with transmission failure. Another Zagato, 0220R, the first one to be built and the 1960 Earls Court car, in which the driving was shared by Mike Salmon and Sir Gawaine Baillie, withdrew at about the same time with piston trouble. Up until then it had been the leading British car.

Essex Racing Stables had continued to campaign its Zagatos actively throughout 1962. Tony Maggs in 1 VEV was third in the GT race at Oulton Park in April, while Jim Clark was fourth in a similar race at Silverstone on 12 May. Later that month its sister car, 2 VEV, was in Belgium participating in the Spa Grand Prix, held on 20 May. ERS had loaned the Zagato to Equipe National Belge for Lucien Bianchi to drive, and it was fitted with a special works 3.7-litre magnesium block engine. There was a tussle with Ferraris for the lead but Bianchi crashed badly on the third lap at the Burnenville curve.

Thereafter 0183R was rebuilt with a new body which was both lower and lighter than the original.

BACK AT THE TT

Both cars were at the 100-lap Tourist Tro-phy race at Goodwood in August, Graham Warner driving 1 VEV and Jim Clark in the reworked 2 VEV. A Zagato, driven by Mike Salmon, completed the trio of DB4 GTs, although none finished the race. Warner withdrew while on only four cylinders, Sal-mon's car succumbed to gearbox trouble and Jim Clark, who had been amongst the lead-ers early on in the race, collided on lap 62 with Surtees' GTO Ferrari at Madgwick and both cars left the road. Fortunately neither driver sustained injury.

The East Hanningfield based Essex Racing Stables once again entered in the Montlhery 1,000-kilometre event in October but Jim Clark and Sir John Whitmore were unlucky in 2 VEV for, after an eventful race, it retired with a holed piston on lap 39. In truth, the Zagatos were coming towards the end of their competitive life and ERS had disposed of both its cars by 1964.

In the meantime, Aston Martin had been pursuing the concept of its Project cars and 212 gave way in 1963 to two new designs: Projects 214 and 215. Once the decision had been made, there was the matter of 212's aerodynamics to be resolved so that the improvements could be incorporated for the 1963 ventures. In September 1962, Richie Ginther drove 212 during an evaluation ses-sion at Silverstone and, in the same month, it was subjected to testing in the MIRA wind tunnel. It was found that at 175mph (281kph) there was about 500lb (227kg) lift under the rear axle. With a full tank of petrol 212 weighed about 1,200lb (544kg) at its back, so down the straight at Le Mans, Hill was losing approximately half his tail-end weight. The rear end of 212's body was therefore redesigned with the flat, so-called Kamm tail and spoiler to produce more downforce.

So much for aerodynamics – Project 214 will be considered first. As the DB4 GT had

been homologated, ingeniously it was decided to use this documentation to allow two so-called 'production' cars to be built which could compete in the World Touring Car Championship and Le Mans.

A PAIR OF 214s

Project 212 had been based on the DB4 GT platform chassis, so there was little more development that could take place. In an effort to save unwanted pounds, this concept was not pursued and a new girder chassis, which was drilled for lightness, was con-structed. As a result, the lighter of the two Project 214s weighed 18.9cwt (962kg), 29lb (13kg) less than 212. This was little less than an exercise in rule bending because the frame bore no relation to that of the produc-tion GT, although fortunately nobody checked! The front suspension was also peculiar to it and was a wishbone and coil layout with standard lower wishbones and short upper ones. As the 214s were ostens-ibly DB4 GTs, the 212's de Dion rear axle was not perpetuated and the production car's twin trailing link and coil-spring lay-out was specified. The live rear axle was a special lightweight 7HA Salisbury unit, narrower and with thicker half shafts. The all-round disc brakes followed the DBR1 pattern.

The homologation documents also dictated that the engine be a wet-sump unit and the rules permitted a 1mm overbore. This there-fore went up to 93mm, which gave 3,749cc. The two cars were allotted chassis numbers 0194 and 0195 and, although their engines were of the same capacity, their heads differed slightly. Number 0194 had straight ports, triple 50 DCO carburettors with 9.15:1 com-pression ratio, while 0195 had a standard GT head, 9.3:1 compression ratio and 45 DCOE carburettors. The output of both of these engines was slightly less than the 212's and they were rated respectively

The DB4 GT Zagato Sanction II

Monday, 22 July 1991 saw the unveiling of four final cars which were allotted the model's remaining and unused chassis numbers, nearly thirty-one years after the Aston Martin DB4 GT Zagato made its 1960 début at the London Motor Show.

The project had been initiated in 1987 by the then Aston Martin joint chairmen, Victor Gauntlett and Peter Livanos. They commissioned Aston Martin specialist Richard Williams to uprate four rolling DB4 chassis to GT specifications which, just like their famous predecessors, were then dispatched to Italy and Zagato's Milan premises. Williams' own original DB4 Zagato (0181) was also sent to the *carrozzeria*, where it was dismantled to reacquaint the Milanese craftsmen with their work of three decades before. Then the quartet of new chassis, which were allocated the dormant chassis numbers of DB4GT/0192, 0196, 0197 and 0198, were bodied anew. They were then returned – resplendent in authentic light green paint – to Williams at his Cobham, Surrey premises, fitted with interiors and completed.

The cars are outwardly identical to their 1960 to 1963 counterparts, although there are a few unobtrusive changes to improve handling and performance. Perhaps the less obvious of these is the most fundamental, for these Sanction II cars have 4.2-litre engines rather than the 3.7-litre ones of the original. They do, however, have the distinctive twin-plug cylinder heads. Experience also showed over the years that the triple Weber 45DCOE4 carburettors performed better with slightly extended inlet manifolds, and these have been fitted. Also, alternators now take the place of the original dynamos. Minor changes have been made to the geometry of the front suspension which has altered the front roll centre to remove bump steer from which the original cars suffered. At the rear, each of the back axles are braced by tubes welded to the nose of the differential which stretch back towards the hubs, the latter having double wheel bearings. Inevitably, modern Goodyear Eagle tyres are used instead of the original Avons, although smaller and wider 15 × 6 Borrani wire wheels are fitted.

It is difficult to believe that this Sanction II DB4 GT Zagato was completed in 1991 as it is outwardly identical to the originals.

The exhaust side of Zagato's engine with the filler for the separate radiator header tank in the foreground. The twin-plug head is fitted with 10mm sparking plugs.

As it should be. The immaculate dashboard of the newly completed Sanction II Zagato.

(Opposite) *The Zagato's superb lines are revealed on this 1991 Sanction II car. One of four built, this is chassis 0196.*

at 310bhp at 6,000rpm, and 300bhp at 5,800rpm. In an effort to improve weight distribution, the engines were moved back by about 8.5in (216mm) in relation to Project 212 and, of course, the production car. Once again the S532 five-speed gearbox was mounted in unit with the power unit in the manner of the GT proper.

BETTER BODIES

When it came to the bodywork, both 214s showed evidence of the lessons learnt on 212. Their noses were elongated and the air intakes reduced in size. They were also lowered by about 8in (203mm) to prevent air from building up underneath while, at their rear ends, they featured the improvements which had been revealed during testing in the MIRA wind tunnel and which had also been incorporated in 212 for evaluation purposes.

The single Project 215 car was produced alongside the pair of 214s and, although it resembled them outwardly, the mechanicals differed radically. At this time Tadek Marek was at work on the next generation of Aston Martin engines, a V8 unit which would eventually appear in a production car in 1970. Marek therefore met with John Wyer, Harold Beach and Ted Cutting to discuss the type of car that Aston Martin might be building in the late 1960s and early 1970s, and this thinking was incorporated into Project 215.

As a result of these deliberations, the car was fitted with all-independent suspension. The front units were essentially the same as the 212's and shared with the 214s. But for the rear, Cutting first looked at the subframe-mounted Jaguar system used on the Mark 10 saloon and E-type, with its fixed-length drive shaft and lower tubular links, but decided that Aston Martin's chassis design would be unlikely to equate with it. Instead he opted for a double wishbone and coil-spring layout which was mounted straight on to the chassis. The bottom wishbone was a wide V and well spread so that loading would be distributed evenly. This took all the braking forces and spring loads. The upper wishbone's role was concerned with ensuring that the road wheels followed their correct paths. The spiral bevel differential unit was developed from one that had been originally designed for the V12 Lagonda. It was thought that such a suspension system would represent the starting point of one which would eventually find its way on to Aston Martin passenger cars, although the replacement of that generation of models would end up with a de Dion rear axle.

TRANSAXLE UNIT

When it came to the location of the gearbox 215, as an official prototype, did not have to follow the unit construction layout of 214. Instead, it was decided to employ the DBR1's CG 537 five-speed transaxle unit even though, it will be recalled, this had not been without its troubles when used with a 3-litre engine – 215 had a 4-litre power unit . . .

As 215 was to be run in the 4-litre Prototype class, its capacity differed from that of 214 and shared the same 96mm bore and 3,996cc of 212. But as there were no homologation constraints about the use of a relatively standard engine, 215's sump was a dry rather than wet sump one. This allowed the twin cam six to be mounted lower and even further back – by about 1.5in (38mm) in the chassis – which in turn meant a lower bonnet line to reduce drag. The frame itself was essentially similar to that used on the 214s and was therefore of drilled square section tubing, although it incorporated an additional central cruciform to stiffen up the structure to meet the demands of the all-independent suspension.

Advanced as this specification was, 215 had its critics, namely Tadek Marek, who was later to comment waspishly that his 4-litre engine had been:

Installed in an abortion which my friend Ted Cutting created, with independent suspension at the rear and was called a '215' car. Actually it was a very good car – it was only difficult to hold on the road!

A TESTING TIME

Work on the more complicated 215 proceeded at a slower rate than on the pair of 214s, and it was not ready in time for the Le Mans testing weekend of 6 and 7 April. The two 214s, however, were and they were accompanied by Project 212 with its revised, aerodynamically improved bodywork. Bruce McLaren was in one of the 214s and succeeded in lapping in 3 min 52.5 sec which was 10.8 sec faster than the best time achieved in the previous year.

During this invaluable evaluation, the 214 design was shown to be flawed in two important respects. First, the radiators gave trouble; they were essentially those used on the DBR1 and were combined water/oil units. Cutting made some quick calculations and decided that the system could be simplified and that the E-type Jaguar radiator would fit. So a visit was subsequently made to Jaguar distributors, Henlys, and just to be on the safe side no less than six E-type radiators were purchased. One was fitted to each of the cars and no more trouble was experienced from that quarter. The other difficulty related to the lightweight 7HA rear axle which was found to overheat. The axles were running temperatures up to 266°F (130°C), and consequently the teeth were stripped off both the crown wheel and pinion. The original axles accordingly were replaced with the older DB4-based 4HA units, and Salisbury efficiently produced the replacements within a month.

The other changes made to the cars after the test weekend were that all three engines – the two 214 ones and the single 215 – were fitted with small throat GT cylinder heads and 50 DCO Weber carburettors. This gave 214 0194 an output of 314bhp and 0195 310bhp, while 215's was 326bhp at 5,800rpm.

Tadek Marek was responsible for preparing the 214 engines, and prior to the race they experienced piston trouble. Marek believed that the pistons were too heavy and their manufacturer, Hepworth and Grandage, agreed but was unable to have new, specially forged ones completed in time for the race because the forging die was not ready. The revised pistons were therefore never fitted and the original cast ones were used instead. Ted Cutting's Project 215 engine did not suffer in this respect because, having a 96mm bore, it was able to use pistons that had been used previously in the DBR2 programme.

LE MANS LAMENT

The 215 was completed just two weeks prior to Le Mans and was to be driven by Phil Hill and Lucien Bianchi, and as it was a prototype it was entered under the Project 215 name. The two 214s ran as DB4 GTs, 0194 being conducted by Bruce McLaren and Innes Ireland, and 0195 by Bill Kimberley and Jo Schlesser.

Theoretically, all three cars had a chance of winning although none of them finished the course. Project 215, even though it was spectacularly fast (it attained 198.5mph (319.6kph) in practice), withdrew after only three hours' running when the bevel gears in the transaxle failed. The reality was that the 3-litre DBR1 gearbox could not cope with the 4-litre engine of 215. It had been a borderline case and Cutting later recognized that he should have used the more robust S532 gearbox from the DBR2.

The pair of 214s lasted longer, but the

engine of the McLaren/Hill car exploded after sixty laps when the top came off a piston. The broken connecting rod nearly cut the sump in half which deposited its entire 3.5 gallons (16 litres) of lubricant all over the track. The other DB4 GT did much better, although it suffered a similar piston failure in the tenth hour. As the leading Grand Touring car, it was lying in third position when it retired on the 146th lap.

The last works Aston Martin entry at Le Mans in David Brown's ownership of the company was in 1963, and the firm did not officially return to the Sarthe circuit until 1989.

Only two weeks after Le Mans, Project 215 was entered in the twenty-five lap GT race held prior to the French Grand Prix at Rheims on 30 June. There was little opposition but, once again, the car suffered from transmission problems. It was driven by Jo Schlesser who lead for the first lap, but he experienced considerable difficulty in changing gear. He missed the cogs on no less than three occasions which saw the engine revs soar to beyond the 6,800rpm mark. Although the engine's bottom end was able to withstand 7,200rpm, this was too much for the valves and they touched, causing them to bend, so that the car had to be withdrawn after completing a mere four laps.

Project 215 also showed itself unpredictable on the fast right-hander after the Rheims pits. Schlesser found the front end too light which suggested that its weight distribution was incorrect – it will be recalled that the car's engine was placed further back in the chassis than both 214 and 212.

BETTER GEARBOX

After Rheims, 215 was rebuilt with the stronger S532 gearbox and Bruce McLaren was due to drive it in the Guards Trophy race at Brands Hatch early in August,

where it was entered with the two 214s. However, McLaren was injured in the German Grand Prix and the Brands Hatch practice session showed that 215 was unlikely to win. Cutting spoke to Wyer and suggested that the car be withdrawn, and instead be taken to Monza in September where the 214s were entered for the Europa Cup. Although it could not run in the race, the high-speed Monza circuit would be an ideal venue to test the car which would have been Aston Martin's 1964 Le Mans entry. Wyer agreed to 215's withdrawal, although eventually it did not go to Monza and, in any event, as McLaren had crashed in the German Grand Prix he would not be able to drive it at Brands. Although the car was withdrawn, Bill Kimberley demonstrated it. Both 214s ran, Kimberley coming sixth in 0194 and Innes Ireland retiring in 0195. As for Project 215, it was subsequently damaged in an accident on the M1, and remained in a dismantled state for some time – it has since been restored.

For the Tourist Trophy race at Goodwood later in August, Aston Martin entered both 214s, their engines now running with forged pistons. Innes Ireland would drive 0194 and Bruce McLaren 0195, but prior to the race John Wyer became embroiled in a wrangle with the RAC over the tyres fitted to the cars. Both 214s had been homologated with 6in (152mm) rims, but since then Dunlop had introduced a 6.5in (165mm) tyre. These tyres were used on the rear wheels and although the cars had been accepted for Le Mans with these wider rims, at Goodwood the scrutineer was insistent that they should run as homologated. This meant changing both the rear axles and brakes as well as the wheels which was particularly galling as Ireland had shared the fastest time of the day with Graham Hill's Ferrari GTO in practice. In the race proper, Ireland was able to challenge Hill briefly in what was to be the winning Ferrari, and he finally came in seventh, having spun on a number of occasions because of the car's narrow section tyres. Bruce McLaren retired with a bent valve after ninety-five laps.

THE TEAM DISBANDS

The 214s were present at the Montlhery Coupe de Paris race on 22 September when, following the retirement of Dauwe's Lotus, the two Aston Martins (driven by Claude Le Guezec and Dewez) came in first and second. The Coupe de Salon saw Jo Schlesser win in 0195 and Le Guezec was placed fifth. This represented the final appearance of the Aston Martin team and the two 214s were sold off at the end of the year to Atherstone Engineering, established by Mike Salmon and Brian Hetreed who were to run the cars as private entries in 1964.

However, the most celebrated performance of a 214 had come at Monza earlier in the month. This was at the three-hour Coppa Inter-Europa event, held prior to the Italian Grand Prix on 8 September. John Wyer later spoke of the race as 'one of the most exciting with which I have ever been concerned'. Roy Salvadori, back with the Aston Martin team for the first time in three years, was in 0194 and Lucien Bianchi was in 0195. Mike Parkes represented the most formidable element of the Ferrari opposition. He was ahead of Salvadori's car from the start but, as the Aston Martin became lighter as it used up its fuel, the gap between them narrowed. Both cars had to stop halfway to refuel which was when 0194 gained eight seconds. This put Roy in the lead, although Parkes moved ahead again, and was once more taken by the 214.

MONZA MAGIC

Salvadori's chance came a couple of laps from the end of the race, when the leaders encountered two cars on the approach to Lesmo. In his own words in *Roy Salvadori Racing Driver*, Roy Salvadori and Anthony Pritchard (Patrick Stephens, 1985) he said:

They obviously had not seen us and I thought if I could scramble past them . . . then Mike would be forced to hold back and take them on the exit. It was a very risky manoeuvre, I eased off a fraction giving Mike the impression that I was going to follow the two other cars through the corner, got my timing to absolute perfection and dived through on the inside.

This caught Parkes off balance and he had to follow the other two cars through the corner. Salvadori went on to win by a mere 100yds (91m) or so, and Bianchi did well to finish third in 0195.

As will have been apparent, and although he was general manager and not team manager, John Wyer fortunately had been present to witness this triumph that represented a fitting note on which to bow out from Aston Martin after thirteen years with the company. Just three weeks after the Monza win, at the end of September, he left the firm to join Ford where he became a key player in its bid to win Le Mans.

His departure was embroiled in the creation of the DB4-derived but flawed Lagonda Rapide luxury saloon. Introduced for 1962, it was the first Newport Pagnell road car to be powered by a 4-litre version of the twin cam six. But only fifty-five were built by the time that manufacture ceased early in 1964 with a fault in the car's de Dion rear axle still unresolved. David Brown had insisted on the car being put into production and this, coupled with his chairman's refusal to sanction an alliance with the Alvis company, culminated in the disillusioned Wyer's resignation.

5 DB5: Objective Achieved

**'Opinions vary greatly – and inevitably – on which is the "best"
of the new breed of Aston Martins. Sir David [Brown]
puts his money on the DB5.'**
Geoff Courtney, *The Power Behind Aston Martin* (Oxford Illustrated Press, 1978).

The Aston Martin DB5, essentially a 4-litre version of the Series 5 DB4, was introduced in September 1963, the month in which general manager John Wyer left Newport Pagnell. The date was not without significance because the car was undoubtedly what Wyer would have wanted the DB4 to have been in the first place.

In the five years since that model's announcement, a considerable amount of all-important development work had been undertaken and the DB5 was fitted with the smoother and more flexible 4-litre engine, which had first appeared in the Lagonda Rapide. More significantly, it was during the model's manufacturing life that Aston Martin turned the financial corner, although profits only remained at around the £3,000 to £4,000 level.

On the international stage, the marque became known to a wider audience when Ian Fleming's hero, James Bond, drove a suitably embellished version in the film *Goldfinger*, released in 1964. As a result, demand for the DB5 was considerable, although it was one which Aston Martin was unable to satisfy.

The DB5 (in factory parlance DP 216) was launched at the 1963 Frankfurt Motor Show which opened on 25 September, the convertible version was unveiled at the Paris Show nine days later, and the definitive coupé was also displayed at that year's Earls Court event.

The London Show car underlined the fact that the DB5 outwardly resembled the Series 5 Vantage DB4 because the appropriately re-engined prototype, DP 216/1, was precisely that. It therefore perpetuated the cowled headlamps introduced on that model, although the Lucas Le Mans-type units were replaced by sealed beam ones from the same manufacturer. Marchal lamps could be specified as an optional extra, and the indicator and sidelights were fitted with a day-night dimmer which was intended to reduce glare to other motorists. Other external differences were the introduction of Sundym tinted glass (previously £15 extra), while the terminal point of the sloping back was extended a further 2in (50.8mm) to the rear of the car.

As already mentioned, the dimensions of the 3,995cc engine were essentially those pioneered in the Lagonda Rapide, and it had also been used in the Project 212 and 215 sports racers. However, the twin SU carburettors of the DB4 were dispensed with and replaced by the Vantage engine's three SU HD8s. The compression ratio was 8.9:1 and the engine was said to develop 282bhp at 5,500rpm although the factory test bed recorded 242bhp.

MORE FLEXIBILITY

The increase in capacity had come because, as Tadek Marek has pointed out:

The DB5 of 1964 was virtually indistinguishable from the Series 5 DB4, which it succeeded, with only the badge on the base of the front wing providing the give-away. They were not, however, fitted to the first few cars.

Having decided that the 3.7-litre engine had more or less reached the limit of its development, we then decided to open it up to 4 litres in production form. In doing this we made two decisions which I think paid off. We decided not to look for top power, we rather preferred to open the curve and get the power in the medium range of revs where it is normally required on the road.

The 4-litre engine with three SUs and the similarly aspirated 3.7 had practically identical power at the top, but there was between 12bhp and 15bhp difference all the way along which, said Marek, gave 'the 4-litre . . . engine much better flexibility and better acceleration'. It also had 'a bit more torque in it, having a much smoother torque curve, was more flexible, and the extra 320cc in

volume helped'. These changes also made the DB5 a slightly faster car than its predecessor with a top speed around the 145mph (233kph) mark.

The most noticeable under-bonnet change on the DB5 was the fact that the valve covers and exhaust manifolds were now stove enamelled. Less apparent were the softer engine mountings. In order to eliminate slight vertical shake, a small hydraulic damper was added to the front of the unit. There was a larger air filter and progressively a Lucas alternator to cope with the additional electrical equipment fitted to the model. The extra power developed by the engine meant that the single plate clutch was replaced by a 9in (229mm) twin Borg and Beck diaphragm unit which had the effect of reducing the clutch pedal pressure

Detail of the DB5's radiator. Note that bumper overriders have now been introduced.

Although the DB5's headlamps resembled those of the last DB4s, which had used Lucas Le Mans components, these were replaced by sealed beam units on the DB5.

The Dunlop chromium-plated wire-spoked wheels with 6.7 × 15 tyres, were carried over from the Series 5 DB4.

A DB5 looking just as good as it did in 1965.

from 43lb to 35lb (19.5kg to 15.8kg). The DB4's clutch had not been for the faint-hearted!

In the first instances there were three different transmission options available on the DB5. First came the four-speed David Brown unit of the DB4 to which a Laycock de Normanville overdrive was available for an extra £72. However, from chassis number 1340, a five-speed German-built ZF gearbox, which was available from the model's outset, became standard equipment. With this unit, top was direct while fifth was geared up to provide an overdrive gear with a ratio of 0.83:1, closely comparing it with the 0.84:1 ratio of the Laycock.

FIVE-SPEED GEARBOX

The gearbox change was made because of troubles that the DB4 had experienced with its clutch and transmission – these would have been compounded on the larger capacity and higher torque engine. Aston Martin would have much preferred to have replaced the David Brown gearbox with a British-built unit but as Harold Beach remembers:

There wasn't a suitable 'box on the British market. I spent a lot of time going to Moss Gears and people like that but as soon as I mentioned the engine torque . . . So the ZF it

The engine of the DB5 was externally similar to the last of the DB4s, although it was of 4 litres, rather than 3.7, and perpetuated the triple SUs of the Vantage-engined DB4.

had to be. The only shortcoming we experienced was that although it was very robust, it had already been used by Maserati [on the 5000 GT] and also a German truck, it was rather noisy when idling. I spent a lot of time with ZF trying to sort it out. It was a question of tuning the centre plate of the clutch to match the characteristics of the gearbox. And we also had a share of clutch problems.

Despite the fact that the twin-plate Borg and Beck diaphragm had been originally specified, this was discontinued for the ZF gearbox and replaced by a Laycock single diaphragm spring clutch.

The third transmission option was a three-speed Borg-Warner automatic, the fitting also having been pioneered on the Lagonda, although it was appearing for the first time on an Aston Martin. The suspension was virtually carried over from the DB4, although on the front the equal length wishbones were modified so that there was a shorter upper one (which followed that used on Project 214) and there was provision to adjust the camber.

Changes were also made to the braking system. Although the all-round discs were perpetuated, they were now Girling rather than Dunlop units and were 11.5in (292mm) in diameter and with a depth of 0.63in (16mm) at the front, and 10.8in (274mm) and 0.5in (13mm) at the rear. The factory claimed that the DB5 could be brought to rest from 100mph (161kph) in six seconds.

Aston Martin was becoming more safety conscious and red lights were introduced on the edges of the doors which illuminated when they were opened. Electric windows, as fitted to the Lagonda Rapide, were perpetuated and the mechanism was intended to start off slowly, accelerate as the glass got to the middle of its travel and slow up again.

Modifications were also made to the heating system which had been a particular bugbear on the DB4. The layout was improved by the introduction of a fresh-air blower in the cold-air ducts, while the flow through the new Smiths heater was said to be 25 per cent greater than that of its predecessor. The car's much criticized controls were replaced by two horizontal levers moving in a quadrant which matched one below it for richening the mixture. The exhaust system was also quietened by the introducton of a second silencer.

AIR-CONDITIONING PLAN

Air-conditioning also became available for the first time on an Aston Martin, although it had been offered on the Rapide. This Normalair system cost £320 extra and, because the only place for the receiver and evaporator was behind the rear seat, this meant relocating the petrol tank. It was replaced by twin, wing-mounted tanks in

The convertible version of the DB4 appeared in 1961 and was continued on the DB5. This left-hand drive example dates from the introductory model year.

The DB5 was what the DB4 should have
been in the first place. Externally identical
to the DB4 Series 5 cars, there were
nevertheless changes below the surface.

(Opposite) Unlike the DB4, the DB5
was fitted with a badge to indicate its
model status.

The DB5's instrument panel was essentially
similar to that of the last of the DB4s and
therefore related to the GT!

the manner of the DB4 convertible, which had the effect of reducing the capacity from 19 to 16 gallons (83 to 73 litres).

Despite the fact that the DB5 was essentially a carry-over from the DB4, the successor cost £4,175 which was £670 more. The price differential between the low-production convertible was maintained and listed at £4,490. In its coupé form the DB5 was over twice the price of Jaguar's E-type, which had appeared in 1961 and which by 1963 cost £1,913. This Coventry-built sports car had successfully challenged the DB4 as Britain's fastest car and was theoretically capable of 150mph (241kph). In truth, this top speed only applied to the carefully assembled press cars, although the Jaguar was consistently faster through all but the lowest gears. Road testers found that the Aston Martin's handling was superior to that of the all-independent Jaguar, but the E-type's ride was superior. It was also 4.3cwt (219kg) lighter than the DB5, although it should be pointed out that the E-type was derived from the Le Mans winning D-type, whereas the DB4 had been conceived, from its outset, as a road car and bore no relation to the DBR1 which had also taken the checkered flag at the Sarthe circuit.

DB5 production began at chassis number DB5C/1251/R, ran to DB5/2275L and accounted for all numbers except for 2021, 2094, 2124 and 2125.

A BOOST FROM BOND

Late in 1963, and therefore early in the DB5's life, the model's reputation received a considerable fillip when Aston Martin

The rear of 007's DB5 featured a 'bullet proof' screen to protect the rear window from gun fire, scythes which emerged from the rear axle and machine guns located behind the rear light clusters. Rotating number plates and extending bumper overriders echoed those on the front of the car.

received a request from film director Harry Saltzman about the possibility of the firm building a special DB5 for Sean Connery as James Bond to drive in the film *Goldfinger*. This was considered by the executive director, Alexander Stuart 'Steve' Heggie, who had taken over the day-to-day running of the factory from John Wyer.

John Wyer's departure had, in fact, given David Brown the opportunity to undertake some reorganization of Aston Martin Lagonda Ltd at board level. Up until then Brown had been both chairman and managing director, but now he shared the latter

position with Jack Thompson from within the Corporation and Steve Heggie was appointed his deputy in August 1963. He had begun his motor industry career with Ford, later moved to Rubery Owen and, from thereon, to David Brown Tractors. Heggie had a particular penchant for publicity and responded positively to Saltzman's approach. The completed car was finished in what Aston Martin called Silver Birch.

The idea was that the film's DB5 would as closely as possible resemble a production car, but that it would be fitted with a number of special features. The car chosen was, in fact, the prototype DB5 – the Series 5 DB4 Vantage which had been displayed on the Aston Martin stand at the 1963 London Motor Show. It bristled with special features which included bumper overriders that could be extended hydraulically to form ramming devices (they were, in fact, actuated by electric motors). Two 'Browning-type machine guns' protruded from the housings for the sidelights which obligingly hinged downwards to let them out. They had to appear to fire and this was achieved by fitting each one with a distributor rotated by its own electric motor which ignited a trickle of acetylene gas.

Each of the rear lamp clusters also contained their own surprises, intended to deter the most ardent of Bond's pursuers. Both could be electrically rotated to reveal, on the left-hand side, a recess which contained about 1pt (56ml) of oil ready to be ejected on the

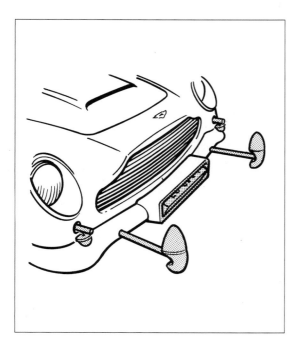

The front of the James Bond DB5 with extended bumper overriders intended for ramming, machine guns concealed behind the side lights and rotating number plates.

road. The right-hand one housed triple-spiked nails which were blown out by compressed air. The nails were not used in the film as it was thought that they might plant undesirable ideas in the minds of small boys!

BEWARE, SMOKE

There was also a smoke-producing device which took the form of a canister of the type used by the Army and discharged into the exhaust tailpipe. In the event of our hero being fired on there was a hydraulically operated (in reality this was electrically activated) 'bulletproof' panel which resided in the boot and could be raised to protect the rear window from gunfire. The windscreen was also said to be bulletproof.

Another memorable feature was the electrically rotating number plates which could be activated when James Bond was making one of his traditionally fast getaways. There were no less than three number plates, two being fakes.

All these desirable 'extras' were fitted to the DB5, although a number of them had to be contrived for the film itself. Perhaps the most celebrated of these was the front passenger's ejector seat. This required the construction of a second car (DB5/1486/R, later registered FMP 7B) which was built with a detachable roof panel. This was an all-important part of the concept so that the hapless, unwanted passenger could be ejected successfully, otherwise he would have been distributed messily around the car's interior. The seat was activated by a button concealed beneath a flip top on the gear lever knob, and this had a special snap-up cover to prevent accidental use.

The seat used for the film was a Martin Baker unit from a fighter aircraft, but unfortunately it took up too much space in the DB5 and also did not look in the least like a car seat. For the actual ejection shot in the film, it was positioned in the Aston Martin

The engine compartment's air outlet duct indicating this version's more powerful Vantage status.

The DB5's rear accommodation was similar to that of the DB4.

The two heater controls were simplified on the DB5 and the one below is for richening the carburettor's mixture. A clock was standard equipment and the radio an extra, the electrics benefiting from the presence of an alternator.

The DB5 looking every inch a thoroughbred. Triplex Sundym windows, previously an extra on the DB4, were fitted as standard.

and then removed and replaced by the original for any further interior shots.

CUT ABOVE THE REST

The driver's seat also had its share of surprises and contained, at its base, a pull-out tray complete with an armoury worthy of a special agent of Bond's calibre. If 007 wanted to contact his boss M, there was also a radio-telephone for such purposes mounted in the right-hand door. The central console was fitted with a radar screen, but in reality this was a convincing looking imitation.

The same went for the chariot-style scythes, which would not have shamed Queen Boudicca, and which were shown in the film emerging slowly from the rear wheel hubs, in order to tear into any other suspicious car which had the temerity to overtake. Their gradual extension was, in fact, effected by trick photography, although the knives existed and ingeniously followed the lines of the triple-eared rear hub caps.

All these modifications added about 300lb (136kg) to the weight of the car, contributions coming from the numerous electric motors, wiring, gas cylinders and the like. These occupied every conceivable nook and cranny and even included the spare wheel well, although what the imperturbable Bond would have done in the event of a puncture is not recorded. The completed car cost around £15,000, or more than three times the price of the standard product.

The premier of *Goldfinger* was held at the Odeon in London's Leicester Square on 17 September 1964, and the film proved to be immensely popular. So many people wanted to see the James Bond DB5 that the film company commissioned a further two duplicate cars from Aston Martin that could be used for publicity purposes. These were numbers DB5/2008/R (which was registered YRE 186H) and DB5/2017/R that carried the BMT 216A number.

THE DB5 IN DEMAND

The screening of the film had an electrifying effect on Aston Martin. As the then service manager, Dudley Gershon, has recounted in *Aston Martin 1963–1972* (Oxford Illustrated Press, 1975):

As soon as the film was shown, a massive wave of publicity hit us, the like of which no other car firm in history had ever experienced.

All of a sudden every ten year old boy knew the name Aston Martin, and this, or else James Bond, was shouted or chalked on every DB4 or DB5 . . . It ran in an amused way through every strata of society, and if we had been able to produce fifty DB5s per week then we could have sold them. Unfortunately, we were just able to do about eleven at that time and we were unable to cash in on the main initial benefit that would have been so easily available. There is a lesson in that somewhere!

The factory produced one more James Bond car, but that was a miniature version of the DB5 convertible, suitably fitted out with the customary 007 goodies for six-year-old Prince Andrew. This was completed in time for a visit, in April 1966, by the Queen and the Duke of Edinburgh to Aston Martin's Newport Pagnell factory and was presented to the royal couple after being demonstrated by Steve Heggie's young son, Iain. Despite instructions to the contrary, but in response to a question from the Queen as to the function of a particular control, he activated it and a group of press photographers standing behind the car were promptly showered with water, much to the amusement of the Duke and, it has to be said, to the representatives of the fourth estate . . .

So much for the special and one-off DB5s; now back to the production cars. In 1965 Aston Martin followed its well-established precedent of offering a Vantage engine to the mainstream model. It was fitted with triple Weber carburettors, flow tuned inlet manifolds to produce a maximum ram effect and a large ported head. The valve timing and distributor setting were also modified, all of which contributed to the declared output of 282bph at 5,750rpm.

THE MODEL EVALUATED

When it came to road test the DB5, *Autocar* managed to secure an example four months before its *Motor* rival, and the latter publication's account did not appear until its issue of 6 February 1965. The car in question was registered DKX 10B (DB/1275/R).

The magazine achieved a speed of 145.2mph (233.6kph) which was over 5mph (8kph) faster than its competitor, who had attained 140mph (225kph). This, *Motor* declared, made the DB5 the third-fastest closed car it had tested – it had only been bettered by the Jaguar E-type and Chevrolet Corvette. The DB5 also achieved the second best acceleration figure to 100mph (161kph) with only the Jaguar being quicker. This meant that the model as *Motor* said:

*In September 1964 came a Vantage version of the DB5, which was
indistinguishable from it, apart from the Vantage name modestly gracing the
bar protecting the air outlet duct. Under the bonnet was a 270bhp triple Weber
carburettored engine.*

*These Touring-bodied Aston Martins have the advantage of looking absolutely
'right' from any angle, as this 1965 DB5 Vantage testifies.*

A three-quarter rear view of the DB5 convertible, a tribute to Aston Martin's Harold Beach, with hood and mechanism by George Moseley.

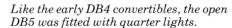

Like the early DB4 convertibles, the open DB5 was fitted with quarter lights.

Rear view of the DB5 convertible with hood neatly stowed.

(Opposite) The front of the DB5 convertible was essentially similar to the coupé.

DB5/1725/R, which The Motor *road-tested for its issue of 6 February 1965, attained a speed of 145.2mph (233.6kph) and a 0–60mph (0–96kph) figure of 7.1 seconds.*

Ranks in the very top bracket of the world's high performance cars. At the expense of a little smoothness, quietness and flexibility, even more performance can be had from the optional Vantage engine . . . Most owners would probably find the less powerful engine best for ordinary road use since it combines to an extraordinary degree those virtues that the other engine is said to partially sacrifice.

Until the oil has circulated properly after its cold start, mechanical noise from the light alloy engine is loud enough to be a little disconcerting, but this quickly dimin-ishes as the engine warms up. Thereafter, throughout a usable rev range extending from idling at 950rpm to 6,000rpm, it is very smooth – especially in the upper reaches to which only the rev counter sets a limit. Unlike competition Aston Martins, which have an unfailing habit of being the noisiest on the track, the DB5 cruises to 100mph (161kph) with absurd ease and quietness and only on hard acceleration does the deep and satisfying rasp of dual exhaust pene-trate loudly inside.

Characteristically instant starting is pro-vided by three HD8 SU carburettors and the sliding choke contol is needed only momen- tarily at its maximum setting. The water thermometer and heater output indicate that the engine does not reach normal oper- ating temperature very quickly but this does not cause hesitancy or jerky pulling when cold, and the tractability is always good. 'Overdrive' fifth gear pulls cleanly from 20mph [32kph] and fourth from about the 15mph [24kph] mark. Using the lower gears the remarkable acceleration figures in the performance data speak for themselves.

On the transmission *Motor* said the following:

The gate for the first four gears is conven- tional, fifth being forward on the extreme right. The lever is spring-loaded in favour of the 3rd/4th plane and has a very small move- ment across the gate so that some drivers did not find the change easy at first, especially when the gearbox oil was cold which made the shift from first to second very stiff. But those who drove the car most were little short of lyrical about the transmission by the time we grudgingly returned the car. A little practice and a quick, firm hand master what soon becomes a particularly easy gear change which, together with delightfully close ratios, inspires frequent use just for the fun of it – especially as, for any given speed between 20 and 100mph [32 and 161kph] there is always a choice of three gears to select. Apart from the straight cut teeth of first which whine slightly, and the gentle sizzle of biting synchromesh, the gearbox is almost silent. So is the rear axle.

Firm, progressive engagement of the large diaphragm clutch has been matched very well to the gearbox and pedal travel is neither too long nor too heavy to prevent the very quick changes that a responsive engine and close ratios demand.

Motor said this on running costs:

With such an expensive car as this, economy is of little more than academic interest and range per tankful is perhaps more relevant than pence per mile. A 4-litre high perform- ance car is inevitably going to be thirsty although good streamlining, high gearing, and a relatively low frontal area keep the DB5's consumption within reasonable limits. Up to almost 90mph [145kph] steady speeds in fifth gear return over 20mpg [14.15l/100km], 31½mpg [8.98l/100km] which, with a 19 gallon [105-litre] fuel tank (including three in reserve) gives an excellent range of 370 miles [595km]. Only unhurried main road journeys, however, are unlikely to give a consumption as high as this, for under normal conditions the car is more often in third or fourth gear than top. Overall con- sumption of 17.6mpg [16.08l/100km] gives a range of 334 miles [537km] . . .

According to *Motor* handling was good:

The rack and pinion steering is very positive and precise and transmits so much feel that it is rather lively on poor roads. Neverthe- less this somewhat vintage character is not all unpleasant and only when parking and turning round sharp corners does it feel heavy. As with all good thoroughbreds response is immediate, and the car can be guided through fast corners with great accuracy, absence of understeer keeping wheel movements down to the minimum one expects of a high geared linkage giving just over three turns from poor lock to lock.

Straight line stability and cornering both reach the high standards expected from Aston Martin with their illustrious competi- tion record. The well-located live rear axle occasionally betrays itself by pattering or jumping sideways when accelerating or cor- nering on a poor surface, but generally the adhesion is excellent and we were fre- quently surprised at just how much power the tyres could transmit without spinning or sliding. Naturally, a heavy right foot will break the back-end away easily on a wet

The famous Aston Martin badge was also duplicated on the cover of the number plate light.

The 4-litre engine of the DB5 convertible.

The DB5 convertible's 'office' was essentially that of the coupé though this example has sensibly not been fitted with a radio. Electric windows are standard.

The DB5 convertible was made in rather larger numbers than the open DB4, with 123 examples built, as opposed to 70 of the previous model.

The convertible's rear seat was slightly narrower than that of the coupé, to allow for the presence of the hood mechanism.

road and correction at the wheel demands a fair amount of precision and (sometimes) strong wrists: the transition from slide to complete adhesion is ill-defined and it's tempting, therefore, to over-correct.

On brakes the magazine said:

The brakes are superb, returning some of the most impressive figures we have yet recorded. After our severe fade test – 20½g stops from over 90mph [145kph] at one minute intervals – there is no increase at all in pedal pressures. Despite a strong smell of hot brake pads, this complete immunity to fade suggests excellent cooling. During maximum stop trials, the drum of our Tapley meter spun farther beyond the 1g mark than we ever remember, an achievement that both the car's testers sensed before they had checked the instrument. This implies not only very well balanced brakes but also outstanding adhesion, confirming our great respect for the Avon GT tyres which are unusually versatile. They are not too harsh at low speeds yet suitable (at slightly raised pressures) for quite long bursts at 145mph [233kph]; they are fairly quiet on coarse surfaces and practically squeal free when provoked; and their adhesion is excellent on both wet and dry roads.

As the data shows, pedal pressures are not high, thanks to servo assistance, but the pedal has such a small travel and thus very little 'give' that the push seems firmer than it is. The fly-off handbrake, working on the rear discs, is not especially powerful and would not hold the car on a 1 in 3 hill. It is just sufficient on a 1 in 4.

Finally, on comfort and control *Motor* had this to say:

Unlike some modern sports and GT cars the DB5 has a traditional firm ride, though we found it neither uncomfortable nor, curiously, out of character with the rest of the car.

Even so, independent rear suspension could undoubtedly allow softer springing without spoiling the handling.

Four damper settings for the rear coil springs are provided by the familiar Armstrong Selectaride system (£12 extra) controlled by a knob on the fascia. The difference between hard and soft is especially marked during fast motorway driving: 'soft' reduced the short but noticeable bouncing of 'hard', an improvement that can actually be heard as the seat cushion almost stops its faint squeak. On ordinary roads under-damping causes a little pitch and wallow that a harder setting completely cures.

The DB5 used new Restall-Keiper seats which, like their predecessors, were adjustable and also hinged forward to provide rear access.

The DB5's instrument panel was essentially that of the Series 5 DB4 though electric windows were standardized with the controls in the centre of the dashboard.

We would not rate the seats amongst the best we have tried though most people found them comfortable enough. There is ample adjustment for reach and the backs are fully reclining, but lateral support – especially on the squab – is poor and beading on the cushion can provide an uncomfortable ridge. However, long journeys did not produce back ache or fatigue and this is a good test of a seat. A thick wood-rimmed steering wheel is set low down in one's lap allowing a very relaxed extended arm driving position. On the non-pendant pedals only the accelerator came in for minor criticism, its strong return spring needing a firm enough pressure to numb the ball of one's foot after some time. Heel-and-toeing is easy.

Unless the front seats are pushed well forward leg room at the back is very cramped and the seats themselves (divided by a central armrest) are fine for children but small for adults.

Motor provided the following table of performance:

Mean of four opposite runs
145.2mph [233.6kph]
Best one-way kilometre
148.2mph [238.5kph]

4th gear (at 5,500rpm)

	122.0mph [193.3kph]
3rd gear	99.5mph [160.1kph]
2nd gear	67.5mph [108.6kph]
1st gear	45.5mph [73.2kph]

'Maximile' speed (timed ¼ mile [0.4km] after 1 mile [1.6km] accelerating from rest)

Mean	132.1mph [212.5kph]
Best	136.2mph [219.1kph]

Acceleration times

0–30mph [48kph]	3.1sec
0–40mph [64kph]	4.2sec
0–50mph [80kph]	5.6sec
0–60mph [96kph]	7.1sec
0–70mph [112kph]	8.8sec
0–80mph [128kph]	11.2sec
0–90mph [145kph]	13.7sec
0–100mph [161kph]	16.9sec
0–110mph [177kph]	22.5sec
0–120mph [193kph]	28.4sec
0–130mph [209kph]	38.1sec
Standing ¼ mile [0.4km]	15.4sec

A FAST ESTATE

The vast majority of DB5s were, inevitably, coupés while the convertible version only accounted for a mere 125 cars. But there was one further variant that had started life as a one-off project for David Brown and which led to the production of twelve replicas. This was the DB5 shooting brake which continued in production into 1966, by which time the model had been replaced by the DB6.

It had been in 1965 that David Brown asked the factory to convert a DB5 coupé into an estate car which meant modifying the rear seating, and adding a roof section and rear opening door. The requirement of this first car was that it should be able to take Brown's polo kit, and should also have a grilled rear compartment for the dogs that had previously delighted in chewing up the expensive leather upholstery of their master's Aston Martins or Lagondas. The first car was constructed by a few master craftsmen at Newport Pagnell with the minimum of drawings and, as a one-off, it was an expensive project to undertake. The car was duly completed and looked very presentable.

There the matter would have rested had it not been for the fact that, at this time, Aston Martin was basking in its post-James Bond glory and David Brown was appearing at numerous public functions, usually in the DB5 estate car, where he was invariably photographed by the press. Before long this publicity began to take effect and Aston Martin began to receive requests for replicas of what was the world's fastest, and most expensive, estate car.

Such a project was far from desirable to the works, and it would obviously have been uneconomic for the firm to have tooled up for such a relatively small production run. The conversion was therefore undertaken by the London-based coach builders, Harold Radford Ltd, and the DB5s were delivered complete to its Hammersmith premises. They were then modified, although Radford subsequently tried to obtain (unsuccessfully as it happened) partially completed DB5 chassis from the factory.

The shooting brake was unveiled at the 1965 Paris and London Shows alongside the DB6, and there were twelve examples excluding the chairman's: eight right- and four left-hand drive cars. Two of the latter were fitted with kilometre speedometers and went to customers on the Continent.

FAREWELL TO FELTHAM

It was during the DB5's manufacturing life that Aston Martin's facilities were all brought under one roof at Newport Pagnell with the closure of the firm's Feltham factory. Despite the fact that all car production had been transferred from there by 1957, the company's Middlesex home had continued to

The DB5, produced between July 1963 and September 1965, was arguably the best of the Marek six-cylinder engined cars.

play host to a number of key activities. The service department was located there and was particularly large, employing about 100 people dealing with around seventy cars a week, with a further sixty in the offing because many Aston Martin owners preferred to have their cars maintained by the factory. In addition, the engineering department had continued at Feltham, while the racing shop had also been so based until the competition programme ceased in 1963. By that time the workforce stood at approximately 150.

Clearly it made sense to have all these activities contained under one roof at Newport Pagnell. David Brown had borne the cost of the Feltham facility, but he eventually agreed to the move in 1963 on condition that each employee would be interviewed to discuss their respective futures. The personnel manager at Newport Pagnell would then be responsible for endeavouring to find local

accommodation and provide assistance for those who made the move. As a result of this dialogue, only thirty Feltham employees elected to stay in the south, the remaining 120 deciding to make the 60-mile (96km) transfer to Buckinghamshire.

These plans were thrown badly off course in January 1964 for, as service manager Dudley Gershon said:

A diabolical rumour was spread, completely unfounded, and which I think was either instigated or else reinforced by an adjacent trading estate coveting the skilled labour, to the effect that David Brown was concentrating the factory at Newport only in order to close it.

As a result of these totally unfounded rumours, only about one-third of those who had intimated that they would make the move, eventually decided to go.

The exclusive DB5 convertible was an expensive car, selling for £4,562 in 1964, which was £314 more than the coupé.

THE MOVE NORTH

The engineering department left in January 1964 and the only people in that section to transfer to Newport Pagnell were Tadek Marek and Harold Beach. The latter says:

This was a great pity because we'd built up an enormous amount of expertise at Feltham but, for instance, many of the ex-Lagonda people had lived in the area for years and didn't want to move. Neither did I! So I commuted from Pinner to Newport Pagnell and I reckoned to have clocked up over a quarter of a million miles [402,325km] on the M1.

The service department was transferred in March, and although of around 100 employees seventy-eight had agreed to make the move, eventually only eighteen actually did so. During a four-week phase-in period, the firm ran buses from Feltham to Newport Pagnell and, by June, that facility was operating at full capacity.

By then, the DB5 had a further eighteen months to run and, by the time that production ceased in October 1965, a total of 1,021 examples of all types had been built. This compared with 1,110 DB4s, although it should be remembered that these had been produced over a five-year period.

However, as the DB5 made way for its DB6 successor at the 1965 Motor Shows, there was a version that was destined to endure for a further year. This was the convertible of which 123 were made and which had been available from the model's outset. Its successor was given the name of Volante and it remained available until October 1966, by which time thirty-seven examples had been made. The model closely resembled the earlier car, and although the rear wings differed, the split bumpers were also related to the concurrent DB6 and the same applied to the trim. It was replaced for the 1967 model year by the DB6 Volante and, as the mainstream model had a longer wheelbase than the DB5's, its predecessor was known as the short wheelbase Volante.

6 DB6: Two Plus Two Equals Six

'In 1958 the DB4 was a trendsetter; 12 years on and vastly
refined, the DB6 retired quietly, almost unmourned.'
Michael Bowler, *Aston Martin V8* (Cadogan Publications, 1985).

When Aston Martin launched the DB6 with its extended wheelbase and improved seating at the 1965 Paris and London Motor Shows, the company had high hopes of increasing production which would help it begin to generate reasonable profits, probably for the first time in its history. These ambitions were dashed by external factors because, in the summer of 1966, the British government introduced a package of swingeing credit controls which depressed the entire British motor industry although, as a vulnerable specialist manufacturer, Aston Martin suffered more than most.

From thereon, DB6 output was running at uneconomic levels and the firm's problems were exacerbated by the expense of having to put the model's DBS replacement into production. This appeared in six-cylinder form in 1967 and, for two years, was built alongside the DB6 until that car ceased production in 1970. From then the DBS was powered by the firm's long-awaited V8 engine.

All these factors combined to place an excessive burden on the David Brown Corporation which was also experiencing its own difficulties so that, in early 1972, and a little over a year since the DB6 had ceased production, Aston Martin was sold.

The origins and evolution of the DB6 are inexorably linked with those of its DBS derivative and that car's V8 engine, and it was, in fact, initially only destined for a two-year manufacturing life. As will become apparent, however, delays in developing its successor resulted instead in it lasting five years.

The beginnings of the DB6 are rooted in an experimental Aston Martin built in 1960. It was in that year that Tadek Marek took a DB4, cut the platform chassis ahead of the heelboard and inserted a new 3.75in (92mm) section of metalwork, so that four rather than two adults could be carried. Titled DP 200/1 and registered 4 YMC, apart from this modification being extended to the roof, its profile was otherwise that of a standard car. Mechanically there were differences from the standard, however, in that it was fitted with a de Dion rear axle and the ZF five-speed gearbox which was to appear in the DB5. A period of extensive road testing then followed, although this 'stretched' DB4 was not tested in a wind tunnel.

It was with this knowledge that in 1964 Aston Martin's product policy meeting decided that the DB5's successor would be a completely new four-seater, wide enough to be powered by the firm's V8 engine which was then under development. This would mean a completely new body which Touring was commissioned to style. Harold Beach began work on a new cruciform chassis and the car was assigned the MP 220 number. It should be made clear that previously Aston Martin schemes, both small and large, had carried the DP, for Design Project, prefix. However, in the late 1950s minor exercises were given their own four-figure numbers

The new split bumper arrangement and oil cooler grille in close up.

(Left) This 1966 DB6 was campaigned in races and hill climbs in the 1970s by its then owner, F.R.C.M. Duret of Weybridge, Surrey.

The rear spoiler made a very real contribution to the DB6's behaviour.

The DB6, as announced in October 1965. Quarter lights were introduced on the coupé. The front was similar to that of the DB5, with the exception of the divided bumper and slats for the oil cooler beneath.

From the rear, the DB6's longer wheelbase and distinctive spoiler are apparent.

while numbers below 1,000 were allotted to all-important designs. This simply succeeded in spreading confusion within the drawing office and, in 1961 and from MP 207, primary studies became Master Projects and the MP letters thereafter replaced the DP ones. After that brief excursion into nomenclature, back to MP 220.

AN ITALIAN JOURNEY

The MP 220's conception meant that the hard-working 4 YMC was effectively sidelined, although road testing continued. In October 1964, 4 YMC was subjected to an extensive 3,492-mile (5,620km) Continental evaluation, fitted with a 4-litre Weber carburettored engine which developed 263bhp at 5,800rpm. While in Italy the Aston Martin party stopped at Weber's Bologna headquarters to have a flat spot attended to, but the principal reason for their visiting the country was to go to Touring's Milan premises to view the 1/10th scale drawing of MP 220. It has to be said that this four-seater coupé lacked the flair of the DB4 and, although well proportioned, it appeared bland and rather anonymous.

The party then returned to Britain and, during the trip, DP 200 recorded a top speed of no less than 158.5mph (255kph) at 6,200rpm and 160.5mph (258.2kph) at 6,275rpm which was the equivalent of flying kilometres of 14.2 and 14 seconds respectively, although there was no reference in the subsequent written report of the all-important road gradient and wind speed tests.

By early 1965, however, the Newport Pagnell team was beginning to rethink MP 220's concept. There were a number of factors for this change of emphasis, in which the car's appearance was a consideration, as was the fact that Touring had been placed under a receivership in February 1965 even though it was continuing to trade. Yet another stumbling block was the tooling costs, which would have been considerable for both a new body and chassis.

Nevertheless, the importance of the concept of a four-seater car was underlined by Aston Martin's marketing adviser who told the company that, in his opinion, all that prevented the DB5 from selling in even larger numbers was the absence of proper back-seat accommodation. If that model's cramped rear compartment could be suitably enlarged, its successor would enjoy a far greater market potential.

In view of these new elements, the concept of 4 YMC was once again reactivated to see if it was viable as a proper four-seater; but with the objective of modifying the roof to increase interior headroom. Therefore, in February 1965, it was tested for the first time in the MIRA wind tunnel, still retaining its mildly modified DB4 roof line. This revealed a disturbing tendency for the car's rear end to lift which was well above the approximate 40lb (18kg) of the then current DB5. This confirmed the impression, already gained during road tests, that the car was less stable at high speeds. Afterwards 4 YMC reverted to its well-established testing role and, from October 1966, was fitted with a de Dion rear axle of the type that was to appear on the impending DBS.

A KAMM TAIL

The starting point of what was to become the definitive DB6 was a DB5 chassis, accordingly lengthened to accommodate four seats and titled MP 219. It was powered by the firm's new V8 engine then under development. However, the body differed from that of its predecessor in that it incorporated a rear spoiler and an abbreviated Kamm tail of that type that had successfully been employed on the Project 214 and 215 sports racers. This car was then subjected to wind tunnel testing and the lift experienced on 4 YMC was cancelled

The cowled headlamps were essentially similar to the DB5. The three-eared hub caps, hitherto an option, were available as a standard fitment.

The DB6's windscreen was more steeply raked than the DB5's at 53 degrees rather than 49 degrees.

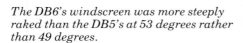

Superleggera badges were fitted to the DB6 until 1967, which was when the Milan company went out of business.

The DB6 was available with the triple Weber carburettored Vantage engine at no extra cost.

Seats were revised on the DB6 to improve comfort.

The DB6's instrument panel was similar in layout to that of the DB5 though the speedometer and rev counter were enlarged while the needles of the auxiliary instruments pivoted at the centre rather than at their bases.

The DB6's heater and carburettor layout were essentially similar to the DB5's.

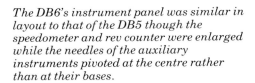

The improved rear seating on the DB6, made possible by a lengthened wheelbase and higher roof. Also note the difference to the pleating of upholstery.

*Above, side view of the DB6. The spoiler's role was to reduce aerodynamic drag
and lift. Below, the DB5-based short wheelbase Volante which was produced for
a year, from October 1965, and ran concurrently with the DB6.*

Aston Martin had already used the Kamm tail to good effect on the Project 215 sports racer of 1963. The concept was later successfully extended to the DB6.

out and replaced by a figure of +10lb (4kg). In addition there was also a reduction in drag, and what was to become the DB6 body recorded a drag coefficient of 0.364, an improvement over the DB4 and DB5 which produced a reading of 0.377. Ironically the best of all figures came from the model of MP 220 which had achieved 0.356. By then it was still being contemplated as the DB6's successor, but what would have been the DB7 was formally rejected at the company's product policy meeting of December 1965, on the grounds of its unacceptable styling.

Work therefore began on the production version of the DB6, which was almost identical to MP 219. Although it had been fitted with a de Dion rear axle, to save tooling costs this was replaced by the live unit of the DB5. Body engineer, Albert 'Bert' Thickpenny, was assigned the task of both restyling the car and re-engineering its structure. This involved altering the windscreen area together with the A Post, bulkhead and door apertures which, with the rear-end modifications, represented the entire body! In the process, and despite the car's extra length, Thickpenny

found that he could obtain a torsionally more rigid structure by substituting box-section cant rails for the DB4 and DB5's Superleggera tubular latticework.

This first car was completed in July 1965, only three months prior to its announcement, and its evaluation was undertaken by research and development engineer, John Haworth. Handling came up to expectations and the improved drag that resulted from the new roof line and spoiler meant that it not only had better acceleration but was also slightly faster than the DB5. That car had been capable of around 145mph (233kph), but the DB6's top speed was approaching the 150mph (241kph) mark, despite the fact that it was about 0.5cwt (25kg) heavier.

LONGER WHEELBASE

The wheelbase of the DB5 was therefore extended by 3.75in (95mm) from 8ft 2in (2,489mm) to 8ft 5.75in (2,584mm). This extra space was inserted just ahead of the rear wheelarches and, with the extra length, it was possible to raise the roof line by about 1in (25mm) to improve interior headroom in the back of the car. A further 2in (51mm) was achieved there by reshaping the rear-seat squabs.

It proved to be rather more tricky to increase the shoulder room as the edges of the rear seats were constrained by the upper of the rear axle's two trailing arms. They were therefore moved back by 3.75in (95.2mm) but were still within the squab area, and the arms were accordingly reduced in length from 17in to 12in (432mm to 305mm) which was to the detriment of the parallelogram created. It did, however, give 4in (102mm) more width, roadholding, Aston Martin assured the press, had not been adversely affected by these suspension changes and rubber bushes took up any conflicting movements.

As a result of these modifications, it was

Looking good: a Mark I Volante with James Bond related number plate!

The wooden body former used to shape the Mark I Volante's tail.

The Mark I Volante shared the DB6's longer wheelbase.

The Volante's ever impressive side profile.

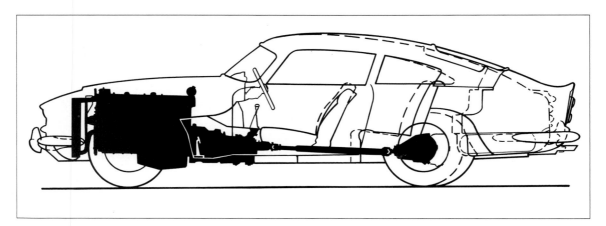

The DB6 differed from the DB4 and DB5 as its wheelbase was 3.7in (95mm) longer to permit improved rear seating. Here its dimensions are compared with its DB5 predecessor.

much easier to carry growing, as opposed to small children and also adults in the back – although preferably those below 5ft 8in (1,727mm) in height. Taller individuals found that their heads were hitting the roof!

The factory had taken note of criticisms of the DB5's seating and Bert Thickpenny was also responsible for redesigning the model's interior, and incorporated suggestions from Steve Heggie and managing director Jack Thompson.

This revamp consisted of changing the shape of the seats to give greater shoulder freedom and better lumbar support, and the pleating used hitherto was replaced by plain squabs. As far as the instruments were concerned, their essential layout remained although the speedometer and rev counter were increased in size from 4in (102mm) to 4.5in (114.3mm), while the auxiliary dials had their needles pivoting in the centre and replaced the quadrant type previously used.

Unlike the DB4 and DB5, the DB6 was fitted with wheel-operated quarter lights in response to customers in hotter countries, and the electrically operated windows of the DB5 essentially were carried over.

A NEW GRILLE

Externally, the front of the DB6 resembled that of its predecessor although a new, horizontally-slatted grille was introduced beneath the front number plate to permit air to reach the oil cooler more easily. Bumpers were also new, and were now divided front and rear, and statutory amber flashing indicators also arrived. The twin petrol filler caps were now fitted with magnetic catches instead of the cable releases that had applied previously. The rear end was, of course, dominated by the spoiler and Kamm tail, both of which were to become the model's most distinctive features.

Mechanicals were much the same as the DB5, although the triple Weber 45 DCO carburettored Vantage engine was a standard fitting. However, the more tractable triple SU carburettored unit could still be specified. Other items which were now included without extra cost were the Powr-Lok limited slip differential, chrome wire wheels and automatic transmission. An electrically operated aerial was also standard, but the radio, which was of the customer's choice, was looked upon as an extra.

4-LITRE DB6

Production	1965–1969 Mark I	1969–1970 Mark II

Engine

Block material	Aluminium alloy
Head material	Aluminium alloy
Cylinders	In-line six
Cooling	Water
Bore and stroke	96 × 92mm
Capacity	3,995cc
Main Bearings	7
Valves	2 per cylinder, dohc
Compression Ratio	8.9:1
Carburettors	Triple SU HD8
Vantage	Triple Weber 45DCOE9
Max Power (net)	282bhp @ 5,500rpm
Vantage	325bhp @ 5,750rpm
Max torque	280lb ft @ 4,500rpm

Transmission

Clutch	Diaphragm spring
Type	Five speed synchromesh on all gears

Gear Ratios

Top	0.83
4th	1.00
3rd	1.23
2nd	1.76
1st	2.70
Reverse	3.31
Final Drive	3.73

Suspension and Steering

Front	Independent, wishbones and coil springs	
Rear	Live axle, trailing links, Watts linkage, coil springs	
Steering	Rack and pinion	
Tyres	6.70–15	8.15–15
Wheels	Dunlop centre lock chromium plated	
Rim size	5.5in	6in

Brakes

Type	Girling disc with separate servos
Size	Front: 11.5in, Rear: 10.8in

Dimensions

Wheelbase	101.75in (2,584mm)	
Track	Front: 54in (1,374mm); Rear: 53.5in (1,359mm)	
Overall length	180in (4,572mm)	
Overall width	66in (1,676mm)	
Overall height	43.5in (1,104mm)	
Ground clearance	53.5in (1,359mm)	
Unladen weight	29.02cwt (1,476kg)	29.5cwt (1,498kg)

An original instruction book and ignition key are desirable aspects of present-day Aston Martin ownership.

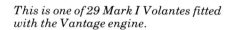

This is one of 29 Mark I Volantes fitted with the Vantage engine.

The all-important chassis plate. The V suffix on the engine number indicates its Vantage specification.

There were the delights of open-air motoring with this genuine four-seater.

The improved DB6 dashboard which served
both the closed and open cars.

The Volante name was the inspiration of
Aston Martin's distribution manager, Kent
Monk.

The Volante featured a new rear number
plate surround with the Aston Martin badge
accordingly relocated.

The boot of the Volante was somewhat
restricted by the presence of the twin,
wing-mounted petrol tanks.

A short wheelbase Volante with its stylish hood raised.

The DB6 sold for £4,998 and was £586 more than the DB5, while the Volante, based on the previous model, sold for the first time at the same price as the coupé.

Chassis numbers began at DB6/2351/R, and ran to DB6/3599/LC and DB6/4001/R to DB6/4081, although these excluded 4039 and 4061. The DB5-based Volante began at DBVC/2301/LN and ran to DBVC/2337/R.

THE DB6 ROAD TESTED

Unlike both the DB4 and 5, the DB6 was tested early in its manufacturing life by the motoring press in view of the uncharacteristically early availability of the model. Neither of the motoring weeklies was, however, able to reach 150mph (241kph), let alone the 160mph (257kph) claimed by Aston Martin. *Motor* published its test in January 1966, recording a speed of 'only' 147mph (236kph) which was put down to possible fuel starvation. However, *Autocar*, whose evaluation appeared in its issue of 25 February, also failed to achieve 150mph and attained 148mph (238kph). Despite this, the DB6 'gave the fastest standing quarter-mile time we have clocked for a four seater, a mean of 14.5 sec'. *Autocar* had this to say about the DB6:

Absolute maximum speeds in the region of 150mph are important as a talking point but somewhat theoretical for most owners. As there is no road or track available with a level measured mile, run-in and braking space for timing two-way high speed dashes,

The Mark I Volante was built between October 1966 and July 1969. No less than 140 were made, more than any other open post-war Aston Martin.

we continue to rely upon our independent electric speedometer. We check results also by calculation against a calibrated tachometer, gear ratios and tyre circumferences with growth allowance.

In the case of this DB6 there is a small but significant discrepancy. The 148mph figure is that obtained, according to our practice, with the aid of a fifth wheel and electric speedometer . . . Using Dunlop R7 racing tyres at 45 psi hot and obtaining 5,825rpm, corrected engine speed, the calculated maximum speed is 150.5mph [242.1kph].

Even more important to owners than maximum speed is the reassuring way the DB6 gives its exhilarating performance. Stability, even when braking hard from high speeds, is exceptionally good, so that

the car is deceptively fast, streaking along at a relaxed 120mph [193kph] as effortlessly as some other powerful cars manage 80mph [128kph]. We had very little difficulty in making several sustained maximum speed runs, because the car is so stable and reaches 140mph [225kph] quickly.

The tandem brake system, with separate servos for front and rear, is one of the most reassuring we have experienced. Rather high pedal loads do not feel high in practice and when making maximum stops the wheels shared the work and positively refused to skid one before another. As a result, the car stopped in a straight line as the tyres 'clawed' it to a standstill. The handbrake, perhaps badly adjusted, would not hold on a 1 in 4 slope.

This Volante is fitted with the triple SU carburettored 4-litre engine used in most of these open cars.

(Left) The vast majority of Mark I Volantes were produced in right-hand drive form and this is another beautifully restored example.

It's that DB6-related rear spoiler again.

For high speed open road touring, the Vantage DB6 is practically ideal. The fifth speed, giving 25.3mph [40.7kph] per 1,000rpm, allows smooth and quiet 100mph [161kph] at only 4,000rpm. There is a certain amount of wind hiss around the quarter light frames and the screen pillars, but no audible transmission or fan noises, and the filtered air intake for the Webers has been silenced effectively. If the accelerator is pressed to the floor a satisfying growl of power is heard from the engine. The exhaust can be picked out only if the windows are open. Aston Martin say that their twin pipe, four silencer exhaust system (which had only limited ground clearance) is very effective in keeping down interior noise.

Owners who expect to do a lot of city and traffic driving would do better to take the standard engine with three SU carburettors. The Vantage engine is not very happy in prolonged jams, becoming fluffy to the ear and lumpy in performance. Even so, we never 'lost' a plug and the engine always cleared after a couple of bursts of power. Bottom gear is high so some clutch slipping is needed to roll along at walking pace. In the first few days the clutch protested malodourously in London, but in the next couple of weeks there was no further trouble.

So far as slow pulling is concerned with the Vantage engine, gentle throttle, which gives ample torque, can be used down as low as 16mph [25kph] in top (4th) – under 1,000rpm, in fact, without snatch – but if the throttles are opened wide below about 2,000rpm the engine gulps and fades. Idling was not very consistent and we had cases of stalling – particularly after a quick stop.

We would prefer the pedal loads to be a lot lighter and the clutch travel shorter. For manoeuvring and parking the steering also feels heavy by current standards, but at high speeds it lightens and becomes just right.

At first we sometimes found second gear hard to locate. The impression is of very narrow slots in the gate which must be selected precisely, and of spring loading towards the opposed centrally positioned 3rd and 4th gear slots. Synchro-bottom is easy to find but there is some resistance to engagement. In other respects it is a nice, very quiet box.

Weight distribution is very nearly 50:50 and the live axle rear suspension is one of the best we have experienced. Adhesion is excellent and, with the Powr-Lok differential, the car will make very quick getaways without twitch or hop.

Even so, practice is needed to get a car like the DB6 away with maximum acceleration. Our successive standing starts got a fraction better and we did some 20 before we were satisfied. Our mean 0–60mph [95kph] figure of 6.5sec is very fast by any standards, as is the standing kilometre time of 25.4sec and we noted that the car reached nearly 130mph [209kph] in a mile. This Aston exceeds 100mph [161kph] in its third, direct fourth and fifth gears, and does over 70mph [113kph] in second, so for overtaking a driver can take his pick according to space and circumstances.

Armstrong Selectaride dampers are fitted which, when set to hard, both stiffen and shorten the suspension movements. The springing is firm, but very stable and comfortable for the type of car. Well padded and bounce-free seat cushions help here, and there was virtually no roll or pitch whatever we did with the car.

Over *pavé* at 25 to 35mph [40 to 56kph] the Aston's suspension was naturally on the hard side for comfort, but the car behaved well. With Selectaride on soft setting the bump stops were reached as the wheels dropped into the worst potholes, but the ride was otherwise more gentle; on harder setting the car was jolted more but did not reach the limits of suspension movement.

The adjustment of the front seat back by knurled wheels gives very fine control of angle – no notches – and our drivers could settle in comfortably. We felt that more curvature behind the shoulders would be an improvement, and those with short legs had to sit close to the steering wheel to reach the full travel of the clutch.

With the front seats set midway on their adjustments, foot and leg room are sufficient for the two rear seat passengers, as is their headroom. In other words, there is enough space there for two, but none to spare. All the occupants enjoy a level ride with virtually no sound coming through from back axle, rear suspension or wheels.

The streamlined enveloping body has not restricted the car's lock which allows an adequate 36.5ft (11.12m) turning circle. Steering is quick, to give instant correction of a rear wheel slide and, when cornering fast, slight understeer experienced with a light throttle changes to slight oversteer when more power is used. For all normal driving the steering characteristics feel neutral and control is very precise. Although the practice is to be avoided with any car, firm braking in the middle of a corner is tolerated by this one without loss of stability. When the car was made to lose adhesion on a skid pad, the slide developed gently and progressively. Occasionally on rough roads the driver could feel some kickback in the steering wheel.

Fuel consumption is not one of the critical considerations for a DB6. On long journeys using 5th gear to cruise at 80–110mph [128–177kph], the car did 15–16mpg [18.87–17.69l/100km]. For short drives in and around London, the figure dropped to 11.5–13mpg [24.6–21.77l/100km]. The large 19 gallon [86-litre] tank, with conventional fillers on both sides of the car, able to take full pressure flow from a pump, was much appreciated on the Continent. The buried fillers have flush flaps to cover them, retained magnetically. A 3 gallon [13-litre] positive reserve is provided which is also appreciated, but we found that it did not always feed when climbing a steep hill.

The interior of the DB6 is well laid out and there is no doubt that top quality materials and equipment are used. On the other hand, the test car was not 100 per cent in every detail of finish around and below the instrument panel. We wondered whether the protruding, though admittedly rounded, boss of the flat steering wheel would increase the risk of injury in a crash, and what the bonnet toggle might do to the driver's knee. Some drivers think that they are getting less than the best if soft flexible vizors are used. They are wrong, but to please them, rigid tinted Perspex vizors are fitted in the DB6 like those of some other top quality cars. Tinted glass is provided all round, anyway, and the rear window contains an effective electric de-misting and de-icing element.

The windscreen is well curved at the edges and the view through is wide and clear. The wiper blades cannot follow the curvature, so rather wide unwiped edges remain. On the test car the blades lifted and chattered at over about 80mph [129kph] and were of little use above that speed. The back window distorts the view in an interesting way, and following cars all looked like GTs a foot lower and two feet wider than life.

Ventilation in summer is assisted by the quarter lights, which have wheels to open and close them, and extractor rear windows. The big main windows are electrically operated. Although the electrical loads must be high to supply all the Aston's equipment, the alternator seems to have no difficulty in coping with them. The heating and fresh air system is the best Aston Martin have produced. The fan is virtually silent and the flow of air can be controlled within fine limits. Separate fresh air scoops supply the front foot wells and each has its own booster fan, but there are no face-level ducts. Full air conditioning can be provided as an extra costing £295, excluding tax.

Autocar said this about the instruments and lamps:

Close-up of the triple SU HD8 carburettors.

A rear view of the same car.

The Volante's distinctive rear trim.

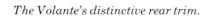

Water and oil thermometers and an oil pressure gauge are supplied, and an oil cooler is standard equipment. The water temperature was always very steady; the oil pressure gauge is of the sensitive kind that moves over a very wide range according to engine speed and temperature.

Thanks to the black leather trim and care in avoiding reflections, the DB6 is a restful car for night driving. The headlamps are very powerful and are dipped by a flick of the lever beneath the steering wheel rim. This is a car which reduces the intensity of its signalling lamps at night, for the benefit of other drivers, particularly those following close behind – a pity so few other cars are likewise equipped.

A number of useful extra lights is provided, one under the engine cover (which is hinged at the front), another in the boot, one in the glove locker where it doubles for map reading, still another flush-fitted in the roof and, that very practical safety feature, automatic red warning lamps in the rear edges of the doors.

Two spare switches are provided, one of which substituted a high pitched wind horn for the normal melodious pair on the test car.

Out-of-the-ordinary details are the provision of fire extinguishers, a plug-in electrical harness and extended tube for the oil dipstick, so you can see where to replace it. The engine itself is attractively finished and keeps nice and clean. Fillers and reservoirs are mounted high and accessibly in a full engine compartment.

This DB6, the most complete Aston Martin built to date, is ideal for Continental journeyings. Reasonably tractable and docile for city driving, it uses no more fuel when cruising at 90mph [145kph] than at 50 [81kph]. It is a commendable attempt to offer the best in motoring – competition performance with carriage comfort.'

This table of maximum speeds was supplied by *Autocar*, and clearly indicates that the DB6 was the fastest model of the range.

Gear	mph	kph
Top (mean)	148	238
(best)	148	238
4th	126	203
3rd	107	172
2nd	74	119
1st	48	77

¼ mile	14.5sec	
1 km	25.4sec	

A DOUBLING OF PRODUCTION?

In addition to having the DB6 in production agreeably early following its announcement, Aston Martin also planned to build it in much larger numbers than its predecessors. Prior to the car's arrival in the autumn of 1965, the factory had only been capable of producing a maximum of eleven cars a week, and it was intended to almost double this figure to twenty without jeopardizing the fact that the Aston Martin was essentially a hand-built car. Dudley Gershon, who had been appointed assistant general manager in 1965 and engineering director in the summer of 1966, was responsible for planning and overseeing these changes. He says:

We began the task . . . by deciding not to alter any of the craft processes. We simply re-allocated some of the work areas and provided extra facilities where we could. We also arranged better balance of the work operations so that more men could work at a stage where this was needed, and we increased the number of assembly stages to facilitate this.

The DB6 had a couple of months to be eased into production so that any problems that might manifest themselves could be ironed out. About the only serious such problem was that some of the first cars showed weakness around the A posts which produced some undesirable door whip, but these were satisfactorily reinforced. For the latter part of 1965, output was running at around the established eleven cars a week but, from then until the end of the third week in each month beginning in January 1966, this was upped by one car a week until June when production stood at an all-time high of eighteen cars a week.

THE NEW TWO-SEATER

Against a background of rising production and a full order book, work began in earnest on the next generation of Aston Martin cars. This was because, as it will be recalled, in December 1965 the policy committee had formally rejected the MP 220 four-seater on grounds of the unacceptable styling of its Touring-designed body. In January 1966 it was decided to commission a supplementary model, what the policy planners at Newport Pagnell called a 170mph (273kph) two-seater. It was obviously incapable of achieving this speed with the current 4-litre twin cam six, but would be wide enough to accommodate the new V8 which was then under development.

Despite Touring's rather lacklustre efforts with the four-seater, the Italian styling house was approached once again to produce a number of studies for what was an out-and-out sports car rather than a Grand Tourer. Designated MP 226, it was decided to base its chassis on a shortened version of the DB6's but with a de Dion rather than live rear axle and a front allied to that of Project 215 with the six-cylinder engine therefore moved back 8.5in (215.5mm). Drawings of this revised platform were dispatched to Touring and the resulting styling studies were received at Newport Pagnell in April 1966.

There were four of them in all, and David Brown opted for one which was also Steve Heggie's choice for, unlike the graceless MP 220, this car's lines possessed all the zest and originality of the DB4. For reasons of security, it was decided that two cars would be built by Touring at Milan and, in May, the two completed chassis – one left-hand drive and the other right-hand drive – were dispatched to Italy. Aston Martin's requirement was that they should be completed in time for the Paris and London Motor Shows of October 1967, a year and a half away.

At this time the bugbear of development costs began to make its presence felt at Newport Pagnell from within the David Brown organization. The assistant general manager, Dudley Gershon, was coming under pressure to dispense with the de Dion concept for this and future projects, and instead revert to the live rear axle of the DB4, DB5 and DB6 family.

A LIVE ISSUE

Gershon therefore 'deliberately "misunderstood" a direct order to ensure that the two chassis for Milan' (from the 1979 Dudley Coram Memorial Lecture) be converted to live axles. 'I knew that I would get accusation of "complicating" the car' and inviting a spate of warranty claims of the sort which had plagued the Lagonda Rapide. To prevent a repetition of that experience, Gershon had 4 YMC dispatched to Inverness and back every day, at an average of 50mph (80kph), using relays of drivers so that the car did about 30,000 miles (48,279km) in a month, almost non-stop, except for one day a week for servicing.

In addition to MP 226, work began on a feasibility study of a widened DB6 in February 1966 which depended, to a greater or lesser extent, on the progress of the long-awaited V8 engine. Sir David Brown has since put that unit into context:

With speeds increasing we decided to embark on the design of a new engine and we decided on a V8, a configuration which was under consideration when we were planning a replacement for the Bentley [designed] six cylinder engine about ten years before. Another reason for designing a larger engine was that we knew Jaguar was working on a twelve cylinder, and the fact that a few American sports cars were appearing with a V8 helped to influence which way we went.

From: *The Power Behind Aston Martin*,
Geoff Courtney
(Oxford Illustrated Press, 1978).

Tadek Marek had begun work on the project in 1963 and the V8 had run for the first time on 29 July 1965. Clearly related to the existing twin cam six, it was an aluminium unit with wet cylinder liners and twin overhead camshafts per cylinder bank. By 1966 its capacity was undecided, although that year Marek revealed:

It could be anything between 4.6 and 5.3 litres . . . At the moment we are working on about 4.8 litres . . . but we don't know what the final volume will be when we put the engine on the market as we intend, somewhere in about two years' time [in fact it was nearer three, for it did not appear until late in 1969, by which time Marek had retired], provided that it gets satisfactory development during the next year.

Marek was concerned that this was:

. . . Going to be much slower at Newport Pagnell than ever it did at Feltham because we lost our machine shop which we had in the experimental department and we gained the so called 'tool room' which is always busy doing production bits. We therefore have to go around the Newport Pagnell area trying to get bits and pieces with which to build an engine.

It was also at about this time (1966) that Dudley Gershon experienced pressure from a source within the David Brown Company, the same one which had advocated scrapping the de Dion rear axle, and which 'was agitating for an American engine to replace the proposed V8 . . . I felt very sensitive over any move to "emasculate" the Aston'.

AN AMERICAN ENGINE?

There was, unfortunately, a precedent for such a course of action. In 1956 Bristol had been developing the new Type 160 3-litre twin overhead six-cylinder engine to replace its BMW-related six, the origins of which were rooted in the 1930s. At this time the firm was owned by the Bristol Aeroplane Company and problems in the aviation world resulted in it being sidelined to save money, and the car company was forced instead to adopt a Chrysler V8 unit. Jensen had also followed suit with its CV8 model. However, the Bristol was a finely engineered Grand Tourer with the accent on refinement rather than performance and had only been in production since 1947. For its part, Aston Martin had a sporting pedigree reaching back to before the First World War and had always been powered by its own, purpose-designed engine.

With the date of the V8's completion still an unknown quantity in 1966, it was also decided to press ahead with the idea of a lengthened DB6 as an interim measure to succeed the current model. This elongated version would use the existing 4-litre six and had its attractions because it was a low-cost exercise which required the minimum of new tooling. The car was based on the fact that the DB6's front essentially dated back to the DB4 of 1958, unlike the rear which had, of course, been redesigned.

A prototype was built, its nose being about 6in (152mm) longer than the DB6's, and it was completed in June 1966. It could have been ready for production by February 1967, in time to be launched at the following month's Geneva Motor Show, but then the doubts set in. The marketing department wondered whether it was sufficiently different from the DB6, and David Brown viewed it and declared himself unhappy with the lengthened front end (which was demanded by the lower bonnet line) which he thought would present owners with a parking problem. In addition, new American safety regulations were due to come into force on 1 January 1968 and the headlamps did not conform to the required height. Relocating them would have meant restyling the front of the car with so-called 'frog eye' protruding headlamps – this would have been visually disastrous. The decision to discontinue the project was taken in early August, and instead the company decided to concentrate on developing a convertible version of the DB6 in time for it to appear at the 1966 Motor Shows.

A WIDER DB6

In the longer term, in late August, thoughts continued on widening the DB6 by about 3.5in (89mm) to accommodate the short but wide V8 engine, and which would have probably taken effect in 1968.

At the same time it was decided to completely restyle the DB6's interior. The job was put out to David Ogle Ltd, the Letchworth, Hertfordshire styling consultants, although the task was simultaneously assigned in-house to William Towns, who had joined Aston Martin late in 1965 with the title of interior styling engineer. Harold Beach puts this appointment into perspective:

We were conscious in the days of the DB6 that we went to enormous lengths to get the mechanicals and appearance of the car right but we really needed someone specifically to style the interior trim. So we advertised for someone and one of the applicants was

William Towns. He'd worked at Rover and I was very impressed with his work and we took him on.

By then Aston Martin was already feeling the effects of a £500 million deflationary package introduced by the government in July 1966. Almost since Harold Wilson's second Labour government had taken office in April 1966, it had made every effort to fend off the spectre of devaluation. By the summer of that year there was a run on sterling and the administration was faced with a stark choice of either having to deflate or devalue. On 20 July, Wilson announced the latter option, although he was eventually forced to devalue in November 1967. The measures included stiffer terms for people wanting to take money out of the country, together with a ten per cent increase on purchase tax and a six-month wage freeze. The motor industry, as an ever-accurate thermometer of the nation's fiscal health, was amongst the first to feel the effects of the moves and output slumped from over 1.7 million cars in 1965 to 1.6 million in the following year. This reflected the fact that all the major car manufacturers had cut back on production, but for a small, vulnerable company like Aston Martin, the effects were little short of calamitous. The cutback was to have far-reaching consequences for the firm and was one of the factors that contributed to David Brown's ceding control of Aston Martin early in 1972.

It will be recalled that production at Newport Pagnell had been running at an optimistic eighteen cars a week in June 1966, but the effects of the government's moves were felt almost instantaneously and Dudley Gershon has recounted:

Our orders were cut back so that, by August, we were in a diabolical position with 130 cars finished at the factory, and on a three day week with production down to ten cars per week.

A SMALL ASTON MARTIN?

The Aston Martin product policy planners recognized that the only answer was to accelerate their engineering programme so that there would be something new to attract public attention before the wider DB6 arrived in 1968. Consideration was also given briefly to producing a pint-sized GT, based on the rear-engined Hillman Imp, which coincidentally was one of the few British cars to also be fitted with a wet liner aluminium engine, the Rolls-Royce Silver Cloud being another. However, Rootes decided to produce the Imp-based Sunbeam Stiletto coupé in 1968 which also incorporated some of the ideas that the Aston Martin team had contemplated, and that put paid to that idea.

More significantly, attention was concentrated on MP 226, the 170mph (274kph) two-seater intended for unveiling in October 1967. Touring was therefore requested to drastically accelerate its schedule to produce the two cars in approximately two months and have them completed by the end of September 1966, rather than a full year later. Although Touring naturally protested at this seemingly impossible deadline, it reluctantly agreed, no doubt in the hope that the car would enter production and so help shore up its increasingly precarious finances. For the vulnerable Aston Martin company, its thinking was that once the car had been shown at the 1966 Paris and London Motor Shows, it could be built in small, hand-crafted quantities alongside the DB6.

In addition to the two-seater Aston Martin, the firm planned to make two further contributions to the 1966 shows. First to be announced was the option of power steering on the DB6, and a ZF unit became available for an extra £125. It was introduced to counter long-running criticism of the car's steering being unduly heavy when it came to parking. It should be noted that Ferrari also introduced the feature on its 330 GT 2 + 2 of the previous year.

A NEW VOLANTE

The second contribution was the convertible version of the DB6 which perpetuated the Volante name. Based on that chassis, it was therefore longer than the DB5-related car that it replaced, and was also distinguished by the fitting of a power-operated hood. It cost £5,594, which was £510 more than the coupé and ran from chassis number DBVC/3600/R to DBVC/3739/R.

Through superhuman efforts, Touring had managed to get the pair of two-seaters completed by the end of September, although the left-hand drive car (266/2/L) was the more advanced of the two. Even so there was no room for a heater and the only way to detach the cylinder head was to remove the engine first. This was because the car had been designed to also accommodate the impending 90-degree V8, so two of the six cylinders were tucked underneath the scuttle. It was intended to put what was to be called the DBS into production in 1967 and the hope was to use as many DB6 components as possible. But examination of the right-hand drive car, 266/1/R, showed that it would take at least six months of engineering and planning to get the model into production.

The left-hand drive car, finished in a 'Black Cherry' hue, was dispatched appropriately to the Paris Show which opened on 6 October, although in view of its incomplete state the doors were kept locked. It looked sensational, with low, stylish lines made possible by the fact that the 325bhp Vantage engine was 2.5in (63.5mm) lower. This required a new sump which was of a similar capacity to the original, as well as being 8.5in (215.9mm) further back in the chassis in comparison with the DB6's. The rear was distinguished by a hatchback which revealed a large luggage compartment with a tool tray and petrol tank beneath. This tailgate was flanked by outlets for an intended sophisticated ventilation system. The car was an uncompromising two-seater with a 'champagne' locker behind the driver's seat which balanced a battery compartment on the other. The DBS was 400lb (181kg) lighter than the DB6 but, at £6,450, was £1,366 more expensive. The Paris event closed on 17 October and the car was subsequently displayed at the London Motor Show which opened on 19 October, although by this time it was sporting new eight-spoked alloy wheels in place of the wire ones which had graced its French début.

GOING TO TOWNS

Because of the amount of work which still had to be undertaken on the car, it was not possible to quote delivery dates at the events, so no orders were taken. This was just as well because, by the last day of the London Show, Aston Martin had decided not to proceed with the two-seater and instead would concentrate its resources on a new car styled by William Towns. Before looking at that all-important project, however, it should be noted that the right-hand drive car (266/1/R), resplendent in 'Dubonnet Rosso' paint, was completed so that it could be displayed at the Turin Motor Show in November. Both cars were then finished off at great expense, registered for the road in 1967 and sold to understanding enthusiasts. For its part Touring finally succumbed to its own insoluble financial problems and closed its doors on 31 January 1967, after forty-one years as one of Italy's most respected styling houses.

What had begun as Town's DB6 interior

Head-on view of a 1968 Mark I DB6. Note that it has lost its Superleggera bonnet badges by this time.

rethink had gathered momentum and developed into a complete car. It will be remembered that Ogle and Towns were to produce their own interpretations of the model's interior – the Letchworth company had borrowed a DB6 from Aston Martin, retrimmed it and both versions were completed by 30 September, although the Ogle contribution was rejected. Harold Beach now takes up the story, for prior to the completion date, 'Towns sat in his office for months . . . designing seats and door trims. But he also used to produce marvellous colour sketches of complete cars like lightning . . . ' Beach then agreed that Towns should officially undertake some of these exterior studies of a widened car, although this had to be done in overtime so as not to jeopardize his work on the interior. There were, in all, three versions all of the same width but with varying wheelbases: a GT described as 'short'; a two-door Aston Martin ('normal'); and a 'long' car which was a four-door Lagonda.

When these sketches were viewed, Beach recognized that Towns 'was in the right place at the right time and when David Brown saw some of the drawings we knew that we'd found a stylist for our new model'. The decision to press ahead with the Towns design was made at an Aston Martin board meeting in mid-October, and an undoubted factor in Brown's approval of the scheme was the possibility of reviving his cherished Lagonda saloon. This decision spelt the end of the two-seater DBS then being displayed at the London Show, although it had certainly attracted plenty of publicity for the marque which was no bad thing . . .

THE £1,000 PRICE CUT

Although work was soon under way on the new model, which was allotted the MP 227 coding, there was still the problem of the sluggish market for DB6s to be resolved. At the beginning of 1967 Aston Martin still had plenty of cars in stock so, in February, Steve Heggie took a calculated risk. The price of the DB6 and Volante were reduced by a £1,000 to £4,067 and £4,577 respectively. This was the equivalent of a twenty per cent price reduction, and David Brown declared: 'We cannot allow stagnation to hold up the development of the considerable potential of Aston Martin Lagonda Ltd'. The hope was that production would rise to the twenty-cars-a-week mark which would have been equivalent to over 1,000 cars a year. In 1967 the company said that it had sold 627 cars, which, it maintained, was thirty per cent more than the 1965 figure. The price adjustment received plenty of press coverage and Dudley Gershon says that, 'a wave of orders wiped out the stock backlog overnight, and it looked as if it would succeed; for a month or so'. The reality that was that, before long, orders began to drop off again and the only thing to do was soldier on until the new car, which was also to carry the DBS name, arrived. It was announced in October 1967, but if it had appeared six months previously, the sought-after higher production rate required by the presence of two rather than one model might have been attained.

BEACH'S DOUBTS

As it was, all available resources were concentrated on the project. Once again Harold Beach was responsible for the chassis and he began work in December 1966. The concept of the MP 227 was, in effect, that of the widened DB6, powered by the V8 engine but with the new Towns-styled body. Beach, however, had reservations about effectively perpetuating the DB6 platform, but he had little choice because of the twin parameters of time and a corporate stipulation that no

(Opposite) *The ultimate version of the line which had begun with the DB4 in 1958, the DB6 Mark II.*

By 1968 the DB6 cost £4,497, though the price had been reduced to £4,068 in February 1967.

unnecessary tooling costs were to be incurred. He says:

My own view is that in the life of any model there comes a time when you have to draw a line underneath it. This should have been done with the chassis of the DB6. No doubt there were cost considerations but we should have designed the DBS on a clean sheet of paper. As it was, the chassis was a carry over from the DB6 and by this time it was too heavy. As always, weight goes up as a model progresses and so it did from the DB4 to the 5 and 6. It was also time to redesign the front suspension that dated back to the DB4.

Nevertheless, Beach was delighted to find that one element of his original DB4 specification, the de Dion axle – the design of which had been exhaustively tested on DP 200 – was destined to appear on the DBS.

For William Towns these were hectic months. The one-third scale clay model was completed by December 1966 and he received the respect of his contemporaries at Newport Pagnell for undertaking his own modelling. Then a one-quarter scale wooden model was needed for wind tunnel testing and there was the matter of the model's interior to be resolved. For this Towns reverted to his original brief of an interior stylist and he produced around five versions of his ideas for the DBSs. It was, however, six months before the final one was agreed by all the interested parties, which ranged from the chairman and directors to their wives.

Body engineering was once again entrusted to Bert Thickpenny and the first prototype DBS was completed on the night of 17 July 1967, just over two months prior to the model's announcement. On the following day of 18 July the car was at the Motor Industry Research Association's establishment near Nuneaton for circuit testing and wind tunnel evaluation. In the latter instance the results were unimpressive. The DBS showed a drag coefficient of 0.416 which compared unfavourably with the DB6's 0.364. This meant that the new V8 would have to develop a minimum of 300bhp, just to match the DB6's performance.

WIND TUNNEL SHOCK

There was also little consolation when it came to the lift figures. Tadek Marek was insistent that, at speeds in excess of 140mph (225kph) the DBS would be unsafe. This was because, at that figure, the car had a 349lb (158kg) lift, against the DB6's 108lb (49kg), while the rear figures were equally discouraging. The DB6 had a downforce of 16lb

(7kg), but the DBS recorded 35lb (16kg) of lift. Modifications were accordingly introduced.

Then there was the matter of the V8 itself which, by the time of the first prototype DBS's completion in July, was in deep trouble. As already mentioned, it was a 90-degree aluminium wet liner unit with twin overhead camshafts per cylinder bank. It had run for the first time in 1965 and gave no trouble on its first test, producing in its original 4.8-litre form 324bhp at 5,750rpm. By June 1965 three V8s were running, two on test beds and one under the bonnet of a modified DB5, later registered NPP 7D. The

The DB5 was first built in rare shooting brake form and the concept was briefly perpetuated on the DB6. Registered YPP 798F, this is one of the examples so converted by Harold Radford.

The new wheels, shod with 8.15 × 15 tyres, were fitted on the Mark II DB6 to make the model appear wider. The triple-eared hub caps were a standard fitment.

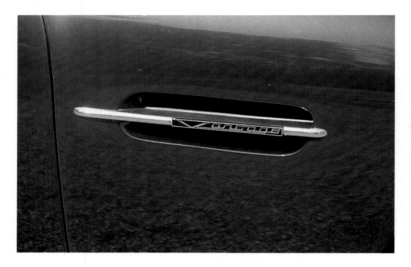

The Vantage engine option was perpetuated on the DB6 Mark II, with triple 45 DCOE Weber carburettors and 9.4:1 compression ratio.

The exhaust side of the 4-litre twin cam six.

*The 1970 Mark II DB6
identifiable by its flared arches
and wider wheels.*

*The petrol filler cap continued to
be located beneath its flap.*

only major difficulty experienced as a result of this evaluation was connecting rod failure. Tadek Marek redesigned them and no more trouble was experienced from that quarter. Three further engines were subsequently built, although when these were stripped down, they revealed problems of a more fundamental nature. There was some evidence of the liners fretting, which had been enough to cause scuffing in their lower block recesses. Marek therefore introduced additional vertical ribbing on the exterior of the block which reduced, but did not totally eliminate the trouble.

At the other end of the engine it was found that the heads were distorting which resulted in gasket blowing, and there was also valve seat distortion. Alan Crouch, who had worked with Marek on the V8 from its outset, recored the head casting and, by October 1966, the trouble was resolved to some extent.

THE V8 AT LE MANS

On the basis that racing would highlight any major defects in an engine, Aston Martin had forged an alliance with Lola. The outcome of this was that two of its rear-engined T70s would be powered by a 5,065cc version of the V8 to be run at Le Mans in 1967. In addition to the capacity increase, these engines were fitted with camshafts of the DB4 GT type, the larger porting and connecting rods being machined from solid which were not dissimilar to those used on the DBR1. These V8s returned about 460bhp at 6,750rpm.

The foregoing problems were of a type that might have been expected during the development of any new engine and bench testing of the basic units continued, as did those being evaluated on the road. Then one of the V8s blew up and it revealed a serious flaw in that it had suffered from main bearing housing failure. Stripping down a

further three V8s confirmed that the problem was not an isolated one. Each of the blocks had incipient cracking around two or more housings and there was evidence of fatigue in others.

First the cap material was changed to Dural, but this was to no avail and there were thoughts that casting faults might be responsible. By this time, however, the 1967 Le Mans race was looming and a calculated risk was taken to go ahead and run the two cars for, despite bench testing, neither block of these modified engines showed any signs of distress.

The race was soon over for the two Lola-Astons. One only lasted for three laps and withdrew with a holed piston, and the other survived for three hours after suffering from numerous engine-related faults, dropping out with severe vibration and low oil pressure. On stripping both engines down, it was found that one had succumbed to the same bearing housing deficiency. By this time there could be little doubt that something was seriously amiss with the engine block and it would require major modification before the V8 could enter production.

By then, however, it was June 1967, the DBS's launch was only three months away and all available resources were concentrated on getting it into production. Any thoughts of fitting the car with the V8 had evaporated and the only answer was to use the DB6's 4-litre Vantage engine. Harold Beach confirms that 'it was never intended to carry over the existing six cylinder engine but we had to have something for the motor show. So we used the six because the eight wasn't ready.'

THE DBS ARRIVES

The DBS was announced in September and it first appeared at the 1967 Paris Show, despite the fact that the transporter delivering the white-finished car crashed *en route*.

The Mark I Volante and DB6 continued in production for 1968 alongside the newly introduced DBS.

It was also displayed at the London Show later in the month. Beach was delighted by Town's styling of the finished product. He says: 'It was the best thing that he ever did. You can put the Touring DB4 and the Towns DBS side by side and forget anything else.'

The only aspect of the design that came in for criticism from those who had created the car was that it was too wide. At 6ft (1,829mm), it was no less than 6in (152mm) more than the DB6 which continued in production and, to give this figure some perspective, that was 1in (25.4mm) more than Rolls-Royce's commodious Silver Shadow saloon.

Sir David Brown voiced his opinion in *The Power Behind Aston Martin*, Geoff Courtney (Oxford Illustrated Press, 1978), when he declared:

. . . it was too big and bulky . . . although it was three inches [76mm] wider than we planned. This is because a mistake was made with the jigs, and when it was discovered that there was a three inch [76mm] difference from the drawings it was too late to change it.

In the same book Harold Beach said that despite his high regard for the car's styling,

The William Towns styled DBS of 1967, based on the DB6 chassis though fitted with a de Dion rear axle and powered by its 4-litre six-cylinder engine.

he and Tadek Marek considered the DBS too wide and unwieldy. However, Beach was able to put the record straight to the present author about David Brown's comments relating to an error having been made in the DBS drawings: 'This wasn't so. [The width] was entirely dictated by the V8 with its two camshafts, plus exhausts and allowances for the front lock.' Dudley Gershon, who as engineering director had overall responsibility for the car, has written that if he had to do the job again, he would have made the DBS about 2in (51mm) narrower. But if the width had been reduced, the car might then have looked too high . . .

WIDE OF THE MARK

The last word on the subject should rightly go to stylist William Towns who has sagely made the point that, because the DBS's width was the same as the projected four-door Lagonda saloon which finally appeared in 1974, it made the Aston Martin appear rather wide for its length. Viewing the Lagonda (of which only seven were built), with its wheelbase 1ft (305mm) greater than the DBS, confirms the point.

At £5,449 the DBS was £1,382 more expensive than the DB6 which continued in production. It was, of course, more luxurious, closer to a four-seater and had better handling on account of its de Dion rear axle. Inevitably, however, its performance, both in terms of its 140mph (225kph) top speed and acceleration, was inferior to that of the DB6 (the engine of which it shared) on account of its extra 3.5cwt (179kg). Output began in earnest in April 1968 and built up slowly to correct any minor difficulties that might have manifested themselves.

With the DBS safely into production, Dudley Gershon found that the concept of scrapping the Newport Pagnell V8 altogether and replacing it with an American unit was reactivated by his Huddersfield masters and has recounted that:

Harold [Beach] and I did some adroit manoeuvring to get this shot down on every count – extra weight, relatively low power of 260bhp maximum, chassis frame and body retooling to accept it – quite apart from the effect on our 'image'.

SINGLE CAM PLAN

Despite the fact that he was certain that the problems with the V8 could be resolved, Gershon and his team were clearly in a weak position because, from the David Brown Corporation's point of view, the idea made good economic sense. Tadek Marek decided

In designing the DBS, Towns had produced a model which was a worthy visual successor to the Touring-styled cars.

to respond to this pressure by proposing a reserve plan, in case the momentum became unstoppable. This was a 'limited power' version of the V8 which could happily retain the then current design by using single cam cylinder heads in place of the twin ones. These would produce more power than the American unit's projected 275bhp but would not unduly stress the potentially fragile block.

Nevertheless, there were thoughts of feasibility trials on the American engine, the Newport Pagnell engineers having already considered and discarded the idea of fitting the 6.2-litre V8 from the Rolls-Royce Silver Shadow. But for Gershon, ' . . . as far as I was concerned it would have been an American cast iron pushrod over my dead body! Aston Martin would have lost in performance and "image" far more than would have been "saved" by a paper exercise.'

There the matter rested until the summer of 1968 which was when Marek retired. Soon afterwards, in early October, Gershon held a crisis meeting with Harold Beach, Alan Crouch and Mike Loasby, who had joined Aston Martin in 1967 and taken over as head of the experimental department on Marek's departure. The group was completed by the presence of engine development engineer, George Evans. The topic was the V8's future and Gershon says that Crouch was authorized:

First, to redesign the cylinder block so that the head studs would be anchored at the bottom deck and feed loosely through at the head face area to relieve it of the present stresses. Second, to follow all stress patterns in the main bearing housing area with stout ribbing, weight to be a secondary consideration, and to redesign the 'caps' . . . Third, to increase the housing areas for the sleeve bottoms. Fourth, to increase the liner seating diameter and its support area both top and bottom, to allow a bore increase to 100mm.

THE V8 SECURE

Alan Crouch had carried out all these objectives by December 1968, and the net result was that the team was able to assemble and run three engines by March 1969, an impressive six months after the crucial autumn meeting. One V8 was built to racing specifications and run unmercifully on the test bed. It was then reduced to road specifications, put into a DBS and subjected to an exhaustive 10,000 miles (16,093km) of running. Then it was removed and replaced by the second engine, and this was followed by the third. All three V8s were then stripped down, and given thorough and exhaustive crack testing and measurement for possible distortion and, says Gershon, 'the result was absolute triumph. We had won, and further tests with more engines failed to throw up a single defect of any sort.' The 5,340cc engine developed 345bhp at 6,000rpm and it was recognized that, with minor modifications, it would withstand 450bhp. With this success, the unit could be installed safely in the DBS and the threat of the American V8 rapidly receded.

From a body standpoint, the DBS's width began to have an adverse effect on the DB6's appearance, as customers started to say that it looked too narrow! It was therefore decided, for purely cosmetic reasons, to replace the 6.70–15 tyres with the DBS's fatter 8.15–15 Avons on 6in (152mm) rims. This involved not only changing the 1.6in (42mm) hubs with larger 2in (52mm) ones but also meant flaring the wheelarches to accommodate the wider tyres.

Despite the fact that William Towns had left Aston Martin in 1968 to pursue what was to prove to be a successful freelance career, his hand was also apparent on the interior of the Mark II DB6 which was retrimmed to more closely resemble the DBS. This included remodelling the front seats along with the rear buckets.

Mechanically, the Mark II was little

The wider wheels of the Mark II DB6 August 1969, proving their worth at Woburn Abbey. Announced in August 1969, the model was distinguished by its flared arches and remained in production until November 1970.

changed from its predecessor; although power steering was standardized. The ZF five-speed gearbox and the automatic transmission were perpetuated, and the choice of standard and triple Weber carburettored Vantage engines continued. There was, however, a new option in the shape of Associated Engineering's Brico fuel injection, which was available for an extra £98.

FUEL INJECTION OPTION

Associated Engineering said that it had spent

seven years developing the system and the DB6 Mark II was the first car to be so equipped. It was an electronic rather than mechanical device with engine conditions and demands conveyed to an on-board computer by five transducers. The claimed advantages were greater flexibility and improved fuel consumption through more accurate monitoring of the fuel and air mixture.

The manufacturer's aim was to ensure 75,000 miles (120,697km) of trouble-free running without attention, other than cleaning the filters to ensure complete reliability.

The variant had a new, rear-mounted badge.

The Mark II's interior was revised by William Towns. Power steering was standard on this model.

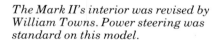

Rear lights were essentially carried over from the DB6 Mark I.

(Opposite) The remainder of the body was unchanged though the ½in (13mm) difference between the front and rear tracks disappeared.

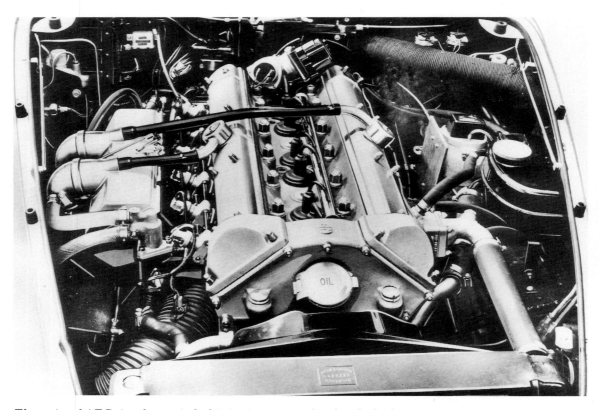

The optional AE Brico electronic fuel-injection system, fitted to the high-compression cylinder head, was introduced on the DB6 Mark II. It was used on forty-six cars though, in practice, the system proved to be unreliable.

As the accent was still very much placed on sales, at £4,833 the DB6 Mark II was £34 less than its predecessor, but with the modifications it meant that it was slightly slower – perhaps by 2mph (3.2kph) – on account of additional wind resistance caused by the wheelarch flares.

The first of the Mark IIs, chassis number DB6 Mk 2/4101/R, was built in July and the model was announced in August 1969. The last of the original DB6s was also manufactured in July, by which time 1,327 had been produced, making it the best selling of the Touring-bodied Aston Martins. This total included six Harold Radford shooting brakes, five of which were left-hand drive cars, and two with Vantage engines. They were all essentially similar to the DB5 version, although Radford managed to incorporate neatly the distinctive DB6 spoiler. The upward-hinging rear door provided excellent access, especially when the two rear seats were folded forward. In addition F.L.M. (Panelcraft) of London converted a further three.

Work was, in the meantime, proceeding on the V8 engine, the DBS V8 being announced in September 1969 and entering production in April 1970. The car was transformed by the arrival of the Bosch fuel-injected 5.3-litre unit which endowed it with a top speed of 160mph (257kph), the magic 100mph (161kph) coming up in a mere fourteen seconds. Once again Aston Martin was making one of the world's fastest cars.

The reason for the DBS's width became apparent in 1970 with the arrival of the 5.3-litre four overhead camshaft V8 engine. The power unit of the renamed DBS V8 was fitted with this Bosch mechanical fuel-injection system from the outset though it was replaced in 1973 by Weber carburettors.

THE V8 IN PRODUCTION

The DBS V8 was almost outwardly identical to the DBS – apart from its cast-aluminium five-stud wheels designed at Newport Pagnell, the model thus becoming the first Aston Martin not to have been fitted with knock-off wire ones. New Girling ventilated disc brakes were also introduced. Transmission was soon replaced by a later version of the durable ZF five-speed gearbox, although a three-speed Chrysler automatic gearbox took the place of the Borg-Warner unit hitherto employed.

The V8 sold for £6,897 which was £785 more than the six-cylinder DBS version which remained in production, and an extra £2,064 on the price of the DB6 which was

similarly perpetuated for a time. The reality was that Aston Martin could not cope with more than one model at a time and the end finally came for the DB6 in November 1970, at chassis number DB6 Mk 2/4345/R. The model had therefore been in production for little over a year, with 245 being built, and the Brico fuel-injection option had proved to be something of a disappointment. There were reliability problems with the system and, of the forty-six cars so equipped, many were converted back to Weber carburettors. The DB6 Volante had ceased production in July 1969 and, with the end of the Mark II coupé, the line which had begun with the DB4 in 1958 was finally extinguished after twelve years.

This was not, however, the end of the road

for the 4-litre six-cylinder engine, as it soldiered on under the bonnet of the DBS, this car remaining in production until May 1972, by which time 829 had been built. It was replaced by the similarly engined AM Vantage, with a revised and rather tidier front end and single rather than twin headlamps. Of the seventy cars built, sixty-eight were powered by the triple Weber carburettored Vantage engine with the remaining two being SU aspirated. With that model's demise in July 1973, production of the long-running twin overhead camshaft aluminium wet liner engine ceased after fifteen years.

ASTON MARTIN SOLD

The firm was, in the meantime, pressing ahead with the development of the four-door version of the DBS and the Aston Martin Lagonda, the marque name having been relegated to a model one – this was unveiled in prototype form in January 1970. Sir David Brown (he had been knighted in the 1968 New Year's Honours List for services for export) was delighted and used the car as his personal transport. It was finally unveiled at the 1974 Motor Show.

By this time Aston Martin was no longer in the ownership of the David Brown Corporation. The car company had never really recovered from the cut-backs of 1966, and the cost of introducing the V8 (the body tooling alone had cost £500,000) placed an additional financial strain on it. As a result, in 1970 Aston Martin recorded a loss of £1,143,388 on a turnover of £2,870,808. Steve Heggie had taken over from Jack Thompson as managing director in 1970, but he left the company and corporation at the end of the year to take up a job with a commercial vehicle manufacturer in America. His place was taken by Malcolm Montgomery from within the David Brown organization.

Despite the fact that British car production

was booming (it rose substantially from 1.64 million in 1970 to 1.74 million in the following year), Aston Martin was in deep trouble. In a bid to spread the crippling tooling costs, methods for substantially increasing production were considered. By this time it was only running at around six cars a week which could have been much more if the V8 engine had been available in larger numbers.

Contemplation was given to upping output to a hitherto unprecedented rate of 100 cars a week, with manufacture being undertaken by outside companies. After these flights of fancy had been discarded, the firm reverted to its established aim of producing the DBS V8, DBS and eventually the Lagonda, with the profitability threshold being crossed when their combined output exceeded twelve cars a week.

This was a future objective but, in an effort to reduce overheads, no less than 230 employees (thirty per cent of the Newport Pagnell workforce) were made redundant in June 1971. Malcolm Montgomery departed late in 1971 after a mere twelve months in office. Turnover dropped to £2,399,756, but losses rose to £1,299,199.

A PAPER PROJECT

It was in this depressing atmosphere that Sir David Brown began to contemplate a new Aston Martin in 1971. Harold Beach says that the chairman 'was very conscious for the need for a completely new car and my idea was to have the transmission in the back in [the later Porsche 928 manner]. It had a target weight of 25cwt [1,270kg], that was about 10cwt [508kg] lighter than the DBS V8, and I intended designing a new platform chassis.' This front V8-engined two plus two had a striking Towns-designed body with gullwing doors, but it only remained a paper project.

Trouble was brewing in another part of the

David Brown organization. The firm had invested heavily in tractor production but this was followed by a slump in sales which produced liquidity problems, and the Huddersfield business was forced to sell off that facility. By early 1972 Aston Martin's accumulated losses were spiralling and, on 16 February of that year, Sir David Brown sold out for a mere £100 to Company Developments Ltd, a Solihull-based property company. The purchase was made on the understanding that the firm would be unencumbered by £5 million worth of bank overdrafts and debts incurred via intercompany loan accounts.

So, after twenty-five years, Sir David bowed out. He had made an immeasurable contribution to the company, revived its sports racing involvement and given the firm the accolade of the World Sports Car Championship. He can be considered to have personally created the concept of the DB2 which, in due course, paved the way to the DB4, DB5 and DB6, and ultimately the V8.

THE NEW OWNERS

Company Developments appeared an unlikely saviour for Aston Martin. The firm was run by William Willson, a forty-four-year-old chartered accountant, who was also a director of the Guardian Royal Exchange Group and the Birmingham Citizens' Building Society. On the announcement of the news, Willson declared: 'The David Brown Corporation has problems which it has been unable to solve. I believe a new broom will have a better chance.' The firm had no experience of the motor industry and its only excursion in the motor trade had been its purchase of the Cheylesmore Garage of Coventry. The new managing director at Newport Pagnell was Geoffrey Fletcher, who had a building trade background.

A condition of the sale was that all the existing directors should resign, and this included Dudley Gershon. Interestingly, he later came to the same conclusion as John Wyer had done when he reflected on the reason for Aston Martin's seemingly insuperable financial problems. Writing three years after his resignation, he declared: 'If asked why we never made a profit, my own opinion now is that we simply never charged enough for the car.'

Company Developments' stewardship of Aston Martin was destined to last for less than three years. Its first move, in April 1972, was to delete the DB initials which had graced all Aston Martins since 1950, the production models becoming the AM V8 and AM Vantage even though Sir David Brown had become the firm's president. Positive achievements were that the V8 passed the all-important American safety and emissions requirements and the Lagonda saloon was launched, although only seven were built. However, fears of asset stripping were confirmed when the firm's collection of old models was disposed of along with ten acres of land adjoining the Aston Martin factory (comprising the firm's playing field and sports club) which were sold for £425,000.

The outbreak of the Arab–Israeli War in October 1973 and the resulting world depression once more saw Aston Martin in trouble. In January 1974 Willson applied, in vain, for government financial assistance and, on 30 December of that year, he declared the firm insolvent. On 6 January 1975 Aston Martin went into receivership, owing Company Developments £750,000. A creditors' meeting was held on 23 January to give the receiver and manager six months to dispose of the business as a going concern.

THE COMPANY SAVED

Thankfully in July 1975 the firm was bought for £1,050,000 by American Peter Sprague, who was head of National Semiconductors in that country, and George

Minden, a Canadian restaurateur and sports car importer. Significantly, both were Aston Martin owners, and they were soon joined by two British businessmen in the shape of Alan Curtis and Dennis Flather. Production restarted in 1976 and, during these years, the V8 models were improved and greatly refined. A new Towns-designed four-door Aston Martin Lagonda saloon arrived in 1976 but did not enter production until 1979.

In 1980 ownership of the firm passed to two shareholders in the shape of Pace Petroleum and CH Industrials, run respectively by Victor Gauntlett and Tim Hearley. Gauntlett, an arch-enthusiast for the products of W.O. Bentley and a keen old-car collector, became the firm's executive chairman late in 1980 and remained so until he resigned in September 1991. In 1983 there was a further chance when Pace's share in Aston Martin was sold to Automotive Investments, the firm's American importers and, in February 1984, it bought out CH Industrials' portion.

Then, in the third and final change of ownership of the decade, Kenneth Whipple, chairman of Ford of Europe, announced at the September 1987 Frankfurt Motor Show that Ford had bought a seventy-five per cent stake in Aston Martin for an undisclosed sum.

The 1988 Motor Show, held at the Birmingham NEC, saw the unveiling of the V8 model's long-awaited replacement in the shape of the Virage, very much in the spirit of its predecessors. Under its bonnet was the greatly refined 5.3-litre V8, now fitted with new thirty-two-valve cylinder heads. After a checkered financial history, Aston Martin, with seventy years of producing some of Britain's outstanding sports cars, now looks well set for the challenges of the twenty-first century.

7 Buying the Right Aston Martin

'Generally speaking, approach second hand cars with grave suspicion.'
Alfred C. Harmsworth, *Motors and Motor Driving* (Longman, 1902).

Because these Aston Martins look so good it is difficult to imagine that there could be anything wrong with them! Potential troubles there are, however, and if you get the wrong car its purchase could turn into a nightmare and a bottomless financial pit. You cannot run a DB4, DB5 or DB6 on the cheap. One of the reasons for this is that, while there are accomplished amateur mechanic owners who are undoubtedly able to tackle most tasks, major jobs do require the attention of a professional specialist. This particularly applies to work on the lovely but delicate six-cylinder twin overhead camshaft aluminium engine, and such work can be costly. Properly looked after, one of these thoroughbreds will provide you with impressive performance and reliability to complement its good looks which are still guaranteed to turn heads.

Before looking at the various models in greater detail, it would be helpful to recap the manufacturing durations of the models in question:

DB4 October 1958 to June 1963: Series 1, October 1958 to February 1960; Series 2, January 1960 to April 1961; Series 3, April to September 1961; Series 4, September 1961 to October 1962; Series 5, September 1962 to June 1963.
DB5 July 1963 to September 1965.
DB6 October 1965 to July 1969.
DB6 Mark II July 1969 to November 1970.

From the 1962 model year all these cars were produced in convertible form, although the Volante name did not appear until October 1965.

I will not deal with the low-production DB4 GT in this chapter because these cars are avidly sought after regardless of their condition, and this applies even more to the Zagato-bodied version which today is a gilt-edged collector's item – and examples change hands for prices in excess of £1 million.

So, let us assume that you are contemplating the purchase of a mainstream model. What are the problems you should be aware of? First there is the all-important matter of bodywork. All these cars have benefited from the use of aluminium coachwork which is a real plus as it cannot rust, although corrosion can be a problem in specific areas. In addition, the DB4 and DB5 were built in accordance with Touring's Superleggera principles, but having said that, the DB6 does not suffer from any particular shortcomings. The bodywork of all models is, in fact, remarkably trouble-free, but even so you should make your first port of call the mounting points of the parallel trailing arms for the live rear axle that you will find ahead of the rear wheel arches. They tend to be rather prone to corrosion. The rubber mounting bushes should, incidentally, be changed at 60,000-mile (96,558km) intervals. While you are in that vicinity, check

An unrestored DB5. The fact that all these cars are fitted with aluminium body panels is an important plus. They are, in the main, trouble-free though they do dent easily.

the rear jacking points as they may be rusted badly; their front opposite numbers can suffer similarly. Also the bottoms of the doors tend to corrode along their edges which is caused when the drain holes become blocked.

RUST IN THE CHASSIS

The platform chassis itself does not suffer greatly from rust with two exceptions – these are the areas immediately adjacent to the bases of the scuttle. To rectify the trouble the bodywork will require surgery and this is a job for the expert.

The heart of the car is, of course, that handsome six-cylinder twin overhead

The post-1963 Aston Martin aluminium wet liner twin-overhead camshaft six-cylinder engines are reliable enough, providing that they are well maintained.

camshaft engine. It will be recalled that the DB4 was powered by a 3.7-litre unit, while the DB5 and DB6 used its 4-litre derivative. Oil pressure is an all-important guide to the engine's overall condition, although when checking this you should first allow the engine to become hot. Up to the Series 3 DB4 of 1961, an acceptable oil pressure reading is 70psi at 3,000rpm. This is because of the early DB4's smaller sump which progressively increased in size until its capacity was standardized at 21pt (12 litres). If you are in any doubt, this important feature was introduced on the Series 2 DB4 at engine number 370/571. Also these early cars have an oil pressure gauge reading of 0 to 100psi while the later ones were graduated from 0 to 160psi.

As these changes were introduced to overcome overheating problems, the advantages of this larger sump hardly needs to be overemphasized. The post-DB4 Series 4 and 5, DB5 and DB6 should have a hot reading of 95psi at 3,000rpm.

You should also be aware of the fact that, until 1962, the DB4 tended to consume oil at rather alarming quantities, although on the plus side practically all of these cars have been modified and fitted with the necessary new piston rings. You should also be aware of the fact that the recommended oil change interval is a brief 2,500 miles (4,023km).

It will be recalled that these aluminium wet liner engines have bleed holes along the carburettor side of the block. If they are weeping coolant this indicates that water has penetrated the usually empty space at the base of the liner, between the upper Neoprene sealing ring and its lower counterpart. A short-term expedient is to add the contents of a tin of Bar's Leak to the water, but this will only work once. If there are signs of leaking, it is a warning that the engine is in need of attention because it means that there is only the lower sealing ring to separate the water from the oil in the sump.

TIME FOR A CHANGE

As these Aston Martin engines feature twin overhead camshafts which are driven by timing chains, these are best replaced at 60,000-mile (96,558km) intervals or when the engine is decoked. This is because the aluminium cylinder block expands when hot and, in turn, stretches the links. You should therefore listen out for noisy timing chains – if this is apparent they will require speedy replacement, otherwise one or other could break and wreck the engine.

On the subject of decoking you should be aware of the fact that unlike some other twin cam engines (the Jaguar XK unit, for instance) there are no shims between valve and tappets to obtain the correct clearance. This is achieved on the Aston Martin six by laboriously grinding the valve stems, or by changing to different-size tappet cups.

The bottom end of the engine is no less sophisticated. The crankshaft runs in seven main bearings. There are three gradings which are accordingly colour-coded, being black, red and green. Crankshaft regrinding is possible to 0.010in and 0.020in. Incidentally, the correct clearance between the bearing surface and the journal is a minute 0.00075in which is required to allow for the inevitable expansion of the aluminium block when hot.

If, by this time, you are under any illusion that rebuilding this engine is a job for the professional, then you will be delighted to hear that the only way to remove the vanadium cylinder liners, which are shrunk into the block, is to steam them out!

Once again the DB4 is the model to avoid when it comes to the transmission. The original Borg and Beck clutch was not really up to its task and has a reputation for heavy operation and rapid wear. The DB5 used a Laycock diaphragm unit while the later six-cylinder DBS of the 1967 to 1972 era employed a Borg and Beck diaphragm. It is worth mentioning that this last unit is by far and away the most satisfactory and can be fitted to the earlier cars with the only modification being a minor one to the release mechanism.

BEWARE OF THE GEARBOX

When it comes to the gearbox, the DB4's David Brown all-synchromesh unit can be regarded as the worst of the lot. The synchro cones tend to wear and can tip off their saddles with the result that the luckless driver is unable to change gear. However, this only occurs when the gearbox oil gets hot, so a quick run around the block will not reveal the problem. A half-hour's drive will be much more telling.

Overdrive arrived as an option on the Series 3 DB4 but the five-speed ZF unit, which appeared on the DB5, was altogether more satisfactory. Although it can be noisy, it is otherwise not prone to any obvious peccadilloes. Borg-Warner automatic transmission was offered as an option from the DB5 onwards, but the 4-litre twin cam six, with its lack of low speed torque, did not take too kindly to being so fettered.

All the cars stop well enough, but the all-round Dunlop discs of the DB4 suffered from rapid wear and also require a surprising amount of pedal pressure. The later Girling units fitted to the DB5 onwards are rather more satisfactory in this regard.

The combination of coil and wishbone independent front suspension and coil-sprung trailing arm live rear axle was essentially unchanged on the DB4, 5 and 6. To ascertain the general state of the car's suspension, press down on the front wings — there should be practically no movement. If there is and the car rebounds, then this suggests that the shock absorbers and perhaps also the springs are in need of replacement. A word of warning though: those lovely aluminium body panels are rather delicate, so bear down with the flat of

your hand with the other on top of it, otherwise you risk denting the alloy. The king pins are fitted with rubber gaiters and these can perish or fracture over the years. If this has occurred, water can enter and accelerate wear on the ball joint and thrust pads.

The rack-and-pinion steering can deteriorate similarly if its gaiter is damaged, and wear can also develop in the rubber mounting bushes. To check this you should place a tyre lever between the rack and the chassis, and see if you can produce any excessive movement.

INSIDE KNOWLEDGE

One of the delights of these Aston Martins is the interiors which are trimmed in the finest quality Connolly hide. Wear does occur here, however, and one of the most common areas is on the offside of the driver's seat. The earlier DB4s had a cloth headlining which tended to soil rather quickly as a result of dirt being drawn through from the boot; a more satisfactory plastic material was subsequently used.

It is also worth noting that the DB5 and DB6 are fitted with electric windows, the motors of which are not noted for their reliability. However, the later the car the more trouble-free the unit is likely to be.

So bearing all these factors in mind, which of these cars, built between 1958 and 1970, represents the best buy? Obviously such factors as mileage, servicing history and the number of owners are all important considerations and there are exceptions to every rule but, in the main, the following will apply. From the foregoing it will be apparent that cars before the Series 5 DB4s are ones to avoid. As general manager John Wyer has conceded, the model was put into production before it was ready and many of its shortcomings simply smack of lack of development.

Therefore, if you are looking for such a car

you should begin with examples produced after September 1962 at chassis number DB4/1001/L. Most cars in this series have the added attraction of being powered by the more potent triple SU carburettored, high compression 266bhp Vantage engine. The option is obviously a desirable fitting throughout the range. It was perpetuated in 314bhp triple Weber carburettored 4-litre form on the DB5 for the 1965 season, and was available in 325bhp state on the DB6 from the model's outset. In every instance the engine number is stamped with an SS suffix to indicate the presence of the Vantage specification.

BEST BUY

The DB5 was effectively a Series 5 DB4 with the larger capacity 4-litre engine, better brakes and, in truth, this is probably the best model of the entire range. Many of the DB4's shortcomings had been resolved, and there was the benefit of the smoother and more flexible larger capacity engine. The same goes to some extent for the DB6's mechanicals, although its longer wheelbase and spoilered body perhaps lacks the flair of its predecessors.

A word about the convertibles. Compared with the closed cars, they are comparatively scarce and have the advantage of outstanding good looks, although they do share the same mechanical problems of their closed equivalents. Obviously their interiors are more vulnerable than the coupés' and, if an example has been neglected and the leather seats have suffered accordingly, then the price should reflect the fact that you will be faced with a substantial retrimming bill.

Undoubtedly, the rarest of these convertibles is the short wheelbase Volante of 1965 to 1966. There were a mere thirty-seven of them – this is because they were built on the last of the DB5 chassis. They were only available for a year from October 1965, and

DB4, DB5 and DB6 Production 1958–1970

1958–60	DB4 Series 1	150
1960–1	DB4 Series 2	350
1961	DB4 Series 3	165
1961–2	DB4 Series 4	230
1961–2	DB4 Series 4 Convertible	30
1962–3	DB4 Series 5	145
1962–3	DB4 Series 5 Convertible	40
		1,110
1959–61	DB4 GT	75
1960–3	DB GT Zagato*	20
1963–5	DB5	898
1963–5	DB5 Convertible	123
1965–6	Volante short wheelbase	37
1965–9	DB6	1,327
1969–70	DB6 Mark II	240
1966–9	Volante Mark I	140
1969–70	Volante Mark II	38
		4,008

* Includes one Bertone-bodied coupé.

are thus contemporary with the longer wheelbase DB6 coupé. The Mark I Volante replacement thereafter conformed to the dimensions of its saloon counterpart.

PARTS AVAILABILITY

What of the all-important matter of spare parts? Owners of these six-cylinder cars have the advantage of being extremely well served. Most DB4 spares – and this includes replacement body panels as well as mechanical parts – are available from Aston Service Dorset Ltd (*see* page 188 for the address). This firm not only caters for the cars of the 1958 to 1963 era, but also carries extensive stocks for the Lagonda-engined cars of the 1948 to pre-DB4 years and the right to remanufacture them as they become obsolete. It is also worth noting that the firm also has a large range of components for the post-DB4 models up to the latest Virage model.

For the DB5 onwards, the spares situation has greatly improved over the past couple of years, and the Aston Martin factory claims to hold 97 per cent of parts. Its address is given below.

DB4 Spares

Aston Service Dorset Ltd
73 Ringwood Road
Longham
Wimbourne
Dorset BA22 9AA

DB5 Onwards Spares

Aston Martin Lagonda Ltd
Tickford Street
Newport Pagnell
Buckinghamshire MK16 9AN

Specialist Garages

As will have been apparent, any work on these cars should only be entrusted to a specialist, and the following firms have experience of the DB4, DB5 and DB6:

Aston Engineering
Lonsdale Place
Rowditch
Derby DE3 3LP

Chapman Spooner Ltd
Unit 7
Middlemore Lane
Aldridge
Walsall WS9 8SP

Goldsmith and Young Ltd
Unit 1D
Quarryfields Industrial Estate
Mere
Wiltshire BA12 6LA

H.W.M. Ltd
New Zealand Avenue
Walton-on-Thames
Surrey KT12 1AT

Ian Mason
Aston Martin Services Ltd
139a, Freston Road
North Kensington
London W10 6TH

JOIN THE CLUB

There is a further important element to DB4, DB5 or DB6 stewardship and that is the Aston Martin Owners' Club. One of the world's oldest one-make car clubs, it was instigated in the mid-1930s by Mortimer Morris-Goodall, known to many of his friends as 'Mort'. As a young man of twenty he had met Bert Bertelli at Feltham and, after his purchase of the LM7 team car, drove 'under works control' in 1933. Although he was unsuccessful on that occasion, he was to compete in an Aston Martin

This DB5's interior trim has been removed. The model was soon fitted with the ZF five-speed gearbox, shown here, which was a great improvement over the original four-speed David Brown unit.

The club also has a very active competition section, the principal event of the year being the St John Horsfall meeting at Silverstone, held in memory of St John 'Jock' Horsfall, that great champion of the marque, who was killed in 1949. The essence of the event is to give members an opportunity to campaign their cars, and there are handicap races so that everyone has a chance. A speed trial and hill climb completes a busy calendar which also includes two *concours d'élégance* events a year.

Today the Aston Martin Owners' Club has a membership of around 3,700. It is open to anyone, whether they are an aspiring, past or present owner, or are just fascinated by the marque. The United Kingdom is divided up into areas, each having its own representative. Around a third of the membership is based overseas and there are active centres on the east and west coasts of America and also in Australia, South Africa and, of course, Continental Europe.

Over the years the club has produced an outstanding magazine, and the beautifully produced, award-winning publication has been under Brian Joscelyne's capable editorship since 1975. It contains an excellent combination of reports on club events and competitions, practical advice and all-important historical articles. Also, every member of the club receives a copy of that invaluable source of Aston Martin lore, the *Register*, which the club publishes at regular intervals. A mine of fascinating information, to which this author readily acknowledges a debt, it has an essential place on the bookshelf of any Aston Martin enthusiast.

Full details of Club membership can be obtained from:

James Whyman (Secretary)
1A High Street
Sutton
Near Ely
Cambridgeshire CB6 2RB

When contemplating the purchase of a used Aston Martin, the presence of trim items, such as this badge, is a consideration.

in every Le Mans until 1939 and appeared for the last time on the Sarthe circuit in 1955. But back in 1935, as a result of providing details of his idea to S.C.H. 'Sammy' Davis, the famed sports editor of *The Autocar*, the latter publicized Mort's initiative in the 3 May and 17 May issues of the magazine. Between twenty and thirty like-minded individuals responded and the veteran racing driver, Charles Jarrott, agreed to be the club's president, a position he held until the outbreak of the Second World War. The momentum was continued after hostilities when the club was revived by Richard Stallebrass and that great Aston Martin enthusiast, Dudley Coram, who became chairman in 1953 and held the position until 1975.

The AMOC can offer technical advice and assistance to members and has a comprehensive library at its Cambridgeshire headquarters, containing workshop manuals for all but the most recent models. Also specialist tools are available for hire, and it goes without saying that these services are of the utmost value to prospective and present owners.

Bibliography

Anderloni, C.F.B. and Anselmi, A.T., *Touring Superleggera* (Autocritica, 1983).

Archer, J., Murray, N., Young, J. and Archer, A., *Aston Martin Register* (Aston Martin Owners' Club, 1988).

Bowler, M., *Aston Martin V8* (Cadogan Publications, 1985).

Courtney, G., *The Power Behind Aston Martin* (Oxford Illustrated Press, 1978).

Donnelly, D., *David Brown's The Story of a Family Business 1860–1960* (Collins, 1960).

Gershon, D., *Aston Martin 1963–1972* (Oxford Illustrated Press, 1975).

Hunter, I., *Aston Martin 1914 to 1940: A Pictorial Review* (Transport Bookman, 1976).

Nixon, C., *Racing with the David Brown Aston Martins, Volumes 1 and 2* (Transport Bookman, 1980).

Wyer, J. *The Certain Sound* (Haynes, 1981).

Index